9 Good Habits
FOR ALL READERS

Authors

Leslie W. Crawford, Ed.D.
Dean of the John H. Lounsbury
  School of Education
Georgia College & State University

Charles E. Martin, Ph.D.
Associate Professor of Early Childhood
  and Middle Grades Education
Georgia College & State University

Margaret M. Philbin, Ed.D.
Associate Professor of Early Childhood
  and Middle Grades Education
Georgia College & State University

ZB **Zaner-Bloser**

Special thanks to these educators who participated in the development of these materials.

Bonnie Lynn Fahning (Bloomington Lutheran School, Bloomington, Minnesota)

David Kreiss (Thomas Creighton Elementary School, Philadelphia City School District, Philadelphia, Pennsylvania)

Connie Longville (Schumacher School, Akron City School District, Akron, Ohio)

Dawn Pittman (Davis Elementary School, Camden City School District, Camden, New Jersey)

Kristin Scherman (Thomas Lake Elementary School, Eagan, Minnesota)

Carol Toussant (West Elementary School, Minerva School District, East Rochester, Ohio)

Geraldine Weems (Williams Elementary School, Austin Independent School District, Austin, Texas)

Photo Research and Art Buying: Denise File, Signature Design

Photo Credits

Cover photography, title page, models by George C. Anderson
p7, Planet Earth Pictures, FPG Intl; p9, John Giustina, FPG Intl; p11, Robert Winslow, Animals, Animals; p12, Yarnell, Intl Stock, (inset); Charles Palek, Animals, Animals; p13, Peter Weimann, Animals, Animals; p14 (red wolf), Mark Newman, Intl Stock, (gray wolf), Tim Davis, PR, Inc; p17, Mark Stouffer, Animals, Animals; p19 (top), David M. Schleser, PR, Inc, (bottom), Gregory Brown, Animals, Animals; p20, Fritz Prensel, Animals, Animals; p21, Jeff Lepore, PR, Inc; p25, Ron Maratea, Intl Stock; p26, Mark Newman, Intl Stock; p27, Stephen J. Krasemann, PR Inc; p28, Scott Wm. Hanrahan, Intl Stock; p31, Jonathan Meyers, FPG Intl; p33, Harvey Lloyd, FPG Intl; pp35, 38, Navaswan, FPG Intl; p36, Robert Frerck; Tony Stone Images; p37, Jeremy Horner, Tony Stone Images; pp41, 44, Haroldo de Faria Castro Cast, FPG Intl; pp43, 45, H. Von Meiss-Teuffen, PR, Inc; p46, Robin Smith, FPG Intl; p49, George Ranalli, PR, Inc; p50, Kent & Donna Dannen, PR, Inc; p51, Mark C. Burnett, PR, Inc; p52, Mark Newman, PR, Inc; p53, David Hiser, Tony Stone Images; pp55, 57, 62, Lawrence Migdale; p59, *Ball Play of the Choctaw-Ball Up* by George Catlin, National Museum of American Art, Smithsonian Institution, gift of Mrs. Joseph Harrison, Jr; p60, Paul A. Souders, Corbis; p61, Mike Greenier Photography; p73, HWR Productions; p79, Gail Shumway, FPG Intl; p103, Telegraph Colour Library, FPG Intl; pp105, 109, Bettmann, Corbis; p107, Richard Nowitz, FPG Intl, (inset); Kevin Laubacher, FPG Intl; p108, Chuck Mason, Intl Stock, (inset), Alexander Tsiaras/Science Source, Photo Researcher, Inc; p110, NASA/Science Photo Library; p113, Lester Lefkowitz, The Stock Market; p115, David Parker/Science Photo Library, Photo Researcher, Inc; p116, Fabian Bachrach; p120, Andrew Olney, Tony Stone Images; p121, Bob Thomas, Tony Stone Images; p122, Science Photo Library, PR, Inc; p125, Chuck Zsymanski, Intl Stock; pp130, 132, 135, 137–140, 145–147, HWR Productions; p143, Martin Rogers, FPG Intl; p144, Paul A. Souders, Corbis; p149, FPG Intl; p. 159, A. Gragera, Latin Stock/Science Photo Library, PR, Inc; p164, Paul Wakefield, Tony Stone Images; p167, © 1979, Daniel Cohen; p173, FPG Intl; p175, Warren Morgan, Corbis; p177, Michael Lewis, Corbis; p178, Bettmann, Corbis; p179, Galen Rowell, Corbis; p180, FPG Intl; p183, Holmes-Lebel, FPG Intl; pp185–188, FPG Intl; p191 (top), Hulton-Deutsch Collection, Corbis, (bottom), FPG Intl; pp192, 195, Hulton-Deutsch Collection, Corbis; p194, Bettmann, Corbis; p197, Patrick W. Stoll, Corbis; p201, Tony Stone Images; p202, Steve Bly, Tony Stone Images; p203, Corbis; p204, National Cowboy Hall of Fame and Western Heritage Center; p214, Leonard de Selva, Corbis; p215, Phil Schermeister, Corbis; pp216, 217, Bettmann, Corbis.

Illustration Credits

pp65, 68–70, Charles Shaw, Craven; pp67, 74–77, Kevin Brown; pp81, 83–86, Vern Edwards; pp89, 91, 92, 94, Charles Shaw; pp97–101, Jason Levinson; p119, Ed French; pp127, 129, 131, Gershom Griffith; pp151, 153–156, Pam Carrol; pp161–163, 168–171, N. Jo Tufts; pp199, 207, 209, 210, Ed French.

Printed in the United States of America

02 03 04 05 (302) 6 5 4 3 2

Table of Contents

Getting to Know the
9 Good Habits
FOR ALL READERS

A habit is something you do over and over until it becomes automatic. In this book, you will learn nine good habits to use when you read. Read the habits below.

Before I Read

1. Check it out!
2. Think about what I know about the subject.
3. Decide what I need to know.

While I Read

4. Stop and ask, "How does it connect to what I know?"
5. Stop and ask, "Does it make sense?"
6. Stop and ask, "If it doesn't make sense, what can I do?"

After I Read

7. React to what I've read.
8. Check to see what I remember.
9. Use what I've read.

Unit 1
Encounters With Wolves
Theme: Animals

In this unit, you will develop these 3 habits for all readers.

Before I Read Habit:
Check it out!

While I Read Habit:
Stop and ask, "Does it make sense?"

After I Read Habit:
Use what I've read.

Learn

In this unit, you will work on three habits—one for before you read, one for while you are reading, and one for after you finish reading. Start with **Before I Read**. Read the habit and strategy. Then read my notes below.

Before I Read

Which **HABIT** will I learn?
Check it out!
If I develop this habit, I can find out something about what I am going to read so that I know what to expect.

Which **STRATEGY** will I use to learn this habit?
Skim the charts or graphs to see what it's about.

My Notes

- Strategy says to skim the charts or graphs to see what it's about.

- I see a table called "Wolves of North America."

- I expect the story to be about two different kinds of wolves.

- I wonder what I'll find out about wolves as I'm reading. Will I find out anything new?

Song at Nightfall

It's just after dark near Yellowstone Lake in Yellowstone National Park. All is still except for the chorus of thousands of frogs. Then your ears prick up. A sound, starting low, then growing in loudness and rising in pitch, reaches your ears. The hair on the back of your neck stands up. A wolf is howling. Soon another wolf joins in, and another, until the forest fills up with the **eerie** sounds.

What Is a Wolf?

Wolves are mammals. A mammal is an animal that has hair, gives birth to live young, and feeds them milk. You are a mammal, too. So are mice, cats, and dogs. In fact, dogs and wolves are closely related. Thousands of years ago, humans came into contact with wolves and **tamed** some of them. They may also have taken in lost wolf pups. However it happened, wolves became domesticated. "Domesticated" means "able to live with and help humans."

Over time, dog species were developed from the wolves. Siberian huskies, Alaskan malamutes, and German shepherds are dog species that look and act a lot like wolves. Wolves and dogs are both carnivores. Carnivores are animals that eat meat. The biggest difference between dogs and wolves is that wolves are wild. They don't depend on humans for any of their needs. Wolves will become unhappy if they cannot roam free.

eerie (eer•ee)—scary and mysterious

tamed (taymd)—trained to accept and live with humans

Now read the habit and strategy for **While I Read**. When you see ②, read my notes in the margin.

While I Read

Which **HABIT** will I learn?
Stop and ask, "Does it make sense?"
If I develop this habit, I will stop now and then to make sure I understand what I'm reading.

Which **STRATEGY** will I use to learn this habit?
Decide whether what I'm reading fits with what I know about the topic.

elk—a large animal with antlers, related to deer

Stop and Ask ②

Does it make sense? Decide whether what I'm reading fits with what I know about the topic.

· · · · · · · · · · · ·

I've heard the word "pack" used about a group of wolves before. Now I know more about what it means. It makes sense that the wolves hunt together if they are hunting a large animal.

Gray Wolves and Red Wolves

Two kinds of wolf are found in North America. The gray wolf is larger. The males can weigh as much as 150 pounds. There are many types of gray wolf, but the main difference among them is the color of their fur. The arctic wolf, even though it is white, is a type of gray wolf. So are the wolves living in Yellowstone National Park. Gray wolves are northern wolves. They live in Canada and in states that border Canada, such as Minnesota and Idaho. Red wolves are smaller. Males may reach 80 pounds. Red wolves live in the southwest United States and in Mexico. In the past, both species lived in much larger areas.

The Pack That Hunts Together Bunks Together

Wolves hunt together in groups called packs. When chasing a large animal like an **elk,** the wolves may space themselves out across a long distance. One wolf starts the chase. Then, as it gets tired, another wolf takes its place. The wolves stay in touch with each other with barks and cries. Eventually, the elk cannot run any more, and the wolves will kill and eat it. ② *Strategy Alert!*

Just as the members of the wolf pack hunt together, they also live together. A pack usually has two to twenty members. A pair of wolves called the **alpha** wolves—the alpha male and the alpha female—leads the pack. Many of the pack members are related to the alpha pair. They may be sons, daughters, sisters, brothers, or grandchildren of the alphas. The alpha wolves usually stay together for their whole lives. They are also usually the only members of the pack that have pups.

An alpha male showing another wolf that he's the leader

alpha (**al**•fuh)—the first letter of the Greek alphabet; the first, or lead, wolf in a wolf pack

Help With the Pups

Although the alpha pair has the pups, the whole pack helps raise them. The pups are born in April or May, just when the weather starts to get warmer. The alpha female finds a narrow cave or ledge in which to give birth. The cave is called a den. The pups stay in the den for the first few weeks of their lives, nursing from their mother. The rest of the pack brings food to the mother during this time. This way, the pups are never left alone. Many other animals might find the wolf pups to be a good dinner, so it is important to protect them.

Gradually, the pups start to eat meat. Pack members bring food for them. Sometimes they even chew the food a bit to soften it for the pups. Some pack members, usually aunt or uncle wolves, baby-sit the pups. They take care of the pups so the alpha female can hunt with the pack. Pups are not full-grown until they are two years old. The pack needs the strong alpha female to return to hunting as soon as she can, so a baby-sitter wolf has a very important job. ❓ *Strategy Alert!*

Stop and Ask ❓

Does it make sense? Decide whether what I'm reading fits with what I know about the topic.

I didn't know this about wolves. It kind of reminds me of when I had a baby-sitter take care of me when my mom and dad had to be away.

Finding a Place in the Pack

As the pups grow, they learn how to hunt. They also learn about their place in the pack. Each wolf in a pack knows exactly which wolf is more important and which wolf is less important. The alpha wolves are the most important. Then there might be a **beta** wolf, the next wolf in line. A few wolves never seem to join a pack or start one of their own. They are called lone wolves.

A mother wolf carries her pup.

Sniff, Wrestle, and Howl

The members of a wolf pack develop close **bonds** and take care of each other. They communicate well, using their excellent senses of touch, smell, hearing, and sight to get their messages across. Wolves are smart and curious. They share their knowledge with other pack members. They mark their territory and other interesting places with scents. They recognize each other by sniffing and making sounds.

Wolves also communicate with their bodies. The tail alone can tell a lot about a wolf's place in the pack and how it is feeling. A wolf with its tail curled around its body is a lower-ranked wolf. A wolf that holds its tail high is a higher ranked wolf. Wolves also wag their tails the way dogs do. Wolves lick, touch, and wrestle to play and to claim their place in the pack. The wrestling may look like fighting, but wrestling wolves don't usually hurt each other.

?️ *Strategy Alert!*

Wolves announcing their location

Wolves bark, whimper, and growl. They also howl. Hearing a pack of wolves howling in full voice is an eerie experience. The sound can sometimes be heard for miles. Wolves howl to announce their location to other members of their pack and to other packs. They can hear other packs from as far as 10 miles away.

Howl Around the Campfire

Howling seems to help the pack have strong ties to each other. And, just like humans enjoy a good sing around the campfire, wolves seem to enjoy a good long howl! The howling of wolves is a scary sound to people. People often think 20 or more wolves are howling when it is really only 6 or 8. That's one of the reasons people have been afraid of wolves, even though they have never been known to attack a person. Wolf **conservationists** believe these beautiful animals are to be respected, not feared. Sometime if you're out camping and you hear wolves howling, gather around your own campfire and join in the song! **?** *Strategy Alert!*

conservationists (kahn•sur•**vay**•shuh•nists)— people who work to protect wildlife

Stop and Ask ?

Does it make sense? Decide whether what I'm reading fits with what I know about the topic.

I know that wolves howl because I've seen that on TV. So it makes sense that they howl for a lot of different reasons.

Wolves of North America

Red Wolf
(Scientific name: *Canis rufus*)

Range (where they live)
Southwest United States, Mexico; reintroduced in North Carolina

Color
Red, gold, brown, reddish-brown

Weight (males are usually heavier than females)
60–80 pounds

Size
2–3 feet at the shoulder

Prey (what they eat)
Rodents, small mammals, deer

Status
Endangered in U.S.

Gray Wolf
(Scientific name: *Canis lupus*)

Range (where they live)
Northern United States, Canada, Alaska; reintroduced in Idaho, Montana, Wyoming

Color
Black, gray, white; often a mix of these

Weight (males are usually heavier than females)
80–150 pounds

Size
3–4 feet at the shoulder

Prey (what they eat)
Rodents, deer, elk, bison

Status
Endangered throughout U.S. except for Minnesota; no need for protection throughout Canada

> Now read the habit and strategy for **After I Read**. Then read my notes below.

After I Read

Which **HABIT** will I learn?
Use what I've read.
If I develop this habit, I will think about how I can apply what I just read to my schoolwork and my life. This makes reading really useful.

Which **STRATEGY** will I use to learn this habit?
Identify the most important ideas.

My Notes

- Strategy says to identify the most important ideas.
- Wolves and dogs are a lot alike.
- Wolves are smart and curious.
- Wolves live in families called packs, and the wolves in the pack help each other get food and raise pups.
- Each wolf knows its place in the pack.

Practice 3 of the 9 Habits

Now it's time to practice the three habits and strategies you learned when you read "Song at Nightfall." Reread the habit and strategy below and then do it!

Before I Read

Which **HABIT** will I practice?
Check it out!
If I develop this habit, I can find out something about what I am going to read so that I know what to expect.

Which **STRATEGY** will I use to practice this habit?
Skim the charts or graphs to see what it's about.

 Use the **Before I Read Strategy Sheet** for "Ghosts in the Twilight" on page 6 in the *Strategy Practice Book* to help you check it out.

Ghosts in the Twilight

The trapper unbuckled his snowshoes. Crossing the floor, he placed a pile of gray pelts onto the counter. (Pelts are the skins of animals.) "I brought in 12 pelts," the trapper said. "Pay up the **bounty,** please!" For many years, the United States government offered a bounty on wolves. It was believed that wolves killed sheep and cattle and might attack people. People had a great fear of wolves and hunted them with the goal of stamping them out. The bounty, plus the fear, worked well. By 1950, no wolves were left living in any state in the United States except Alaska. It was a **twilight** of the wolves.

Over time, and on their own, wolves have returned to some areas. Today, a small number of red wolves lives in the southwestern United States. A larger population of gray wolves has moved down from Canada into northern Michigan, Minnesota, and other border areas. But wolves are still absent from most of the places where they had lived in the past.

bounty (bown•tee)—a payment for killing a certain animal

twilight (twie•liet)—a period of decline

A professional hunter/trapper

Remember the *Strategy Alerts!* in **While I Read** in the last selection? They reminded you to decide whether what you were reading fit with what you know about the topic. Now do the same thing with this selection.

While I Read

Which **HABIT** will I practice?
Stop and ask, "Does it make sense?"
If I develop this habit, I will stop now and then to make sure I understand what I'm reading.

Which **STRATEGY** will I use to practice this habit?
Decide whether what I'm reading fits with what I know about the topic.

Use the **While I Read Strategy Sheet** for "Ghosts in the Twilight" on page 7 in the *Strategy Practice Book* as you read.

Threatened, Endangered, Extinct

organisms (**or**•guh•niz•uhmz)— living things

species (**spee**•sheez)— particular type of animal or plant

Many plants, animals, and other **organisms** on Earth are in trouble. As people move into more and more areas of the earth, the life that already exists there has three possibilities. One is to learn to live with people. For example, many birds are easily able to live in cities and neighborhoods. Another possibility is to move. Sometimes, however, there is no place to move. For example, an animal that lives on the shore may not be able to move inland when people build houses on the beach. A third possibility is that the **species** may become extinct. Extinct means that no more individuals of that species are alive.

Each species has a special role to play in its community. Losing a species through extinction is a loss for the whole community it lived in. That's why scientists and governments get involved. Scientists have come up with two names for species that are in trouble—endangered and threatened. Endangered means a species is in danger of becoming extinct if something is not done. Threatened means that the species is at risk of becoming extinct; its future is uncertain.

We tend to think of such animals as reptiles, amphibians, fish, birds, and mammals when we think of endangered species. But many species of plants and **fungi** are also endangered or threatened. In many cases, these species provide the food for animals. Losing a plant or fungus species to extinction can cause problems for many other species. ❓ *Strategy Alert!*

One endangered plant is the Nellie Cory Cactus.

The Endangered Species List

Whether a species is endangered or threatened is a decision that scientists make. Whether a species gets put on the endangered species list is a decision that **lawmakers** make. Usually, the lawmakers discuss the species with scientists and follow their advice when making the decision. This list names all the species that are protected by law in the United States. The law is called the Endangered Species Act. This act tells how species may be chosen for the list and how they are to be protected. It also gives the **penalties** for harming a species that is on the list. The U.S. **Environmental** Protection Agency keeps track of the list.

The manatee is one endangered animal.

Stop and Ask ❓

Does it make sense? Decide whether what I'm reading fits with what I know about the topic.

fungi (**fun**•jie)—a group of lower plants, such as mushrooms, mold, and mildew

lawmakers (**law**•may•kurz)—people who are elected to offices and make laws for a country, such as senators and representatives

penalties (**pen**•uhl•teez) —punishments, often a payment of a fine

environmental (en•vie•ruhn•**men**•tl)— having to do with Earth's natural resources

healthy (**hel**•thee)—large enough to keep the species alive

Stop and Ask

Does it make sense? Decide whether what I'm reading fits with what I know about the topic.

Once a species is put on the list, a plan is made to protect it. The number of individuals of the species is checked regularly. If the plan works and the number goes up, the species may be removed from the list. This is called delisting a species. An example of a delisted species is the American alligator. American alligators were almost extinct. Because of the protection they were given by being on the endangered species list, there is a **healthy** number of individuals today. The American alligator was delisted when scientists thought that the species was no longer threatened. ⁇ *Strategy Alert!*

The American alligator

What About Wolves?

Are wolves endangered? Under U.S. law, they are. The number of wolves inside the borders of the lower 48 states is very, very low. However, if you look outside our country's borders, gray wolves, at least, are not endangered. Canada never had a bounty program for wolves. Healthy numbers of wolves live there. Moving Canadian gray wolves to Yellowstone National Park brings them back to the United States, where they were absent, but the gray wolves do not need protection to keep the species from becoming extinct.

So the Canadian gray wolves in Yellowstone are not endangered. That means that they are not protected in the same way that an endangered species is protected, even though, in the United States, they are in need of protection. The placement of Canadian gray wolves in Yellowstone brings up a question that has never been asked before. Is a species protected because of what it is or because of where it lives? ⁇ *Strategy Alert!*

Stop and Ask

Does it make sense? Decide whether what I'm reading fits with what I know about the topic.

Natural vs. Introduced

For example, if a Canadian wolf crosses over the border into Montana, it is considered to be endangered in the U.S., and it is protected. But the wolves in Yellowstone are not completely protected. They were brought in from an area where their numbers were good. They did not move into Yellowstone on their own, so they are not endangered. Thus, they may be shot under some conditions. A wolf that kills farm animals may be shot, but only if it is one of the **reintroduced** Canadian wolves. A "natural" wolf is completely protected. Anyone killing a wolf that is in the area on its own could be arrested.

How do you tell the "natural" wolves from the "introduced" wolves? It's hard. Court cases are in the process of answering this question. It is hoped that a compromise can be reached. A compromise is a settlement where each side gets something it wanted, but each side also gives up something it wanted. In a compromise, the groups who are arguing agree to follow a common plan.

The red wolves introduced into North Carolina also cause **controversy**. However, that species is more clearly in danger of becoming extinct, even in the areas where they were captured. Thus, they are clearly protected under the Endangered Species Act.

? *Strategy Alert!*

reintroduced (ree•in•truh•**doost**)—a species returned to an area where it was absent

controversy (**kahn**•truh•vur•see)— a situation in which different opinions are strongly held

Stop and Ask ?

Does it make sense? Decide whether what I'm reading fits with what I know about the topic.

A gray wolf pack in winter

Questions About the Future of the Wolves

The future of the gray wolves in Yellowstone is in doubt. Packs are settling into homes there, but they may still be removed. Canada will not take the reintroduced wolves back. If they are removed, they would either be killed or placed in zoos.

The American Wolf—Endangered or Not?

Natural Wolves	Introduced Wolves
A Canadian gray wolf that crosses the border into the United States is considered endangered.	A Canadian gray wolf that is introduced in the United States by humans is not considered endangered.
A Canadian wolf that crosses the border into the United States is completely protected by law.	A Canadian wolf that is introduced into the United States by humans may be shot if it kills farm animals; it is not completely protected by law.
There are no "natural" red wolves in North Carolina, so they are considered endangered.	All red wolves in North Carolina were introduced there, so they are completely protected by law.

Remember that you're not finished until you've used what you've read.

After I Read

Which **HABIT** will I practice?
Use what I've read.
If I develop this habit, I will think about how I can apply what I just read to my schoolwork and my life. This makes reading really useful.

Which **STRATEGY** will I use to practice this habit?
Identify the most important ideas.

Use the **After I Read Strategy Sheet** for "Ghosts in the Twilight" on page 8 in the *Strategy Practice Book* to help you use what you've read.

Apply 3 of the 9 Habits

> Now read "Hunters in the Shadows" and apply these three habits and strategies.

Before I Read

Which **HABIT** will I apply?
Check it out!

Which **STRATEGY** will I use to apply this habit?
Skim the charts or graphs to see what it's about.

While I Read

Which **HABIT** will I apply?
Stop and ask, "Does it make sense?"

Which **STRATEGY** will I use to apply this habit?
Decide whether what I'm reading fits with what I know about the topic.

After I Read

Which **HABIT** will I apply?
Use what I've read.

Which **STRATEGY** will I use to apply this habit?
Identify the most important ideas.

 Use the **Self-Assessment Sheet** for "Hunters in the Shadows" on pages 9–10 in the *Strategy Practice Book* as you read to see how well you can apply the habits and strategies.

Hunters in the Shadows

The ranger puts the walkie-talkie to her mouth and pushes down the button. "We're all ready here. All quiet," she says in a quiet voice. She takes one more look around the fenced pen. The dark green fir trees whistle softly in the early morning breeze. A V of geese, headed north, crosses the clear blue sky. A whisper comes over the walkie-talkie. "On my mark—three, two, one, now!"

The ranger focuses her **binoculars** on the animals on the far side of the snow-covered, acre-wide pen. The pack is resting, but alert. They know something is going on. Slowly, a section of fence is rolled back. The largest of the gray-black animals pricks its ears, then stands. Carefully, it goes to the opening in the fence. It sniffs all around the opening, peeks outside, and is gone. The ranger wipes away a tear. For the first time in 50 years, wolves are free in Yellowstone National Park.

binoculars
(buh•**nahk**•yuh•lurz)
—a hand-held instrument used with two eyes to make faraway things look closer

Return of the Wolves

Until a few years ago, the sight and sound of wolves was missing from Yellowstone. Park workers were trying to return Yellowstone to the way it was in the early 1800s, before many people visited the area. They succeeded in bringing back almost every species but one. There were no wolves. The park was like a jigsaw puzzle with one piece missing. In 1995, wolves were reintroduced, or brought back, to Yellowstone. Now Yellowstone could be seen as a complete puzzle again.

A Yellowstone elk

interactions
(in•tur•**ak**•shuhnz)—
the way things work
together

Role of Wolves

An ecosystem is made of all of the living and non-living things in an area and their **interactions**. Every part of an ecosystem is important. Plants use sunlight, air, water, and parts of the soil to make food. Some animals, such as grasshoppers and elk, eat the plants. Other animals eat animals. Finally, there are animals and bacteria that eat dead or decaying stuff. In a healthy ecosystem, it is important for each species to eat or to be eaten! When one part of the chain is missing, the ecosystem is upset.

bison (**bie**•suhn)—large, shaggy-headed mammals living in the western United States

Wolves are predators. Predators are animals that hunt and eat other animals. In Yellowstone in the past, wolves ate large animals, such as **bison** and elk, as well as smaller animals, such as mice. When the wolves were gone from Yellowstone, the number of elk rose. They ate plants faster than the plants could grow back. The elk became hungry and sick. Predators such as wolves were needed. Wolves tend to attack and kill sick or injured elk, which helps keep the elk herd healthy. It also helps keep the number of elk from growing faster than the plants do. This controls the elk population. Wolves help keep the ecosystem of Yellowstone balanced.

Wolf Arrivals

The wolves that were returned to Yellowstone were found in Canada. They were given drugs to make them sleep and then flown to their new home in the park. For the first few months, the wolves lived in a large pen. About an acre of land was fenced in at several places. This gave the wolves time to recover from their trip and to get used to their new home. The wolves didn't hunt. Instead, park employees fed them. They gave the wolves the **carcasses** of animals found within the park, the same food they hoped the wolves would hunt when they were free. And finally, in January 1995, that day came. The gate was opened. The wolves were free.

carcasses
(**kahr**·cuhs·uhz)—dead bodies

A red wolf being reintroduced into North Carolina

For and Against the Wolves

Many people are happy that the wolves have been returned to Yellowstone. Others, however, have a different view. They oppose the reintroduction of wolves for many reasons. The issue is complicated.

One Side of the Coin

For many people, the day the wolves were freed was a wonderful day. They were excited about truly **restoring** the ecosystem in the park. They felt as if they were making up for all the wolves that had been needlessly killed for bounty in the 1800s.

Many people, too, are worried about the number of species that are becoming extinct. Many scientists think that for an area to be healthy, it should have biodiversity. Biodiversity is the number of different species in an area. Wolves were very nearly extinct in the United States. Restoring wolves to Yellowstone will let the species live on.

restoring
(ri·**stor**·ing)—returning something to the way it was

Another Side of the Coin

Other people were upset that the wolves were reintroduced to Yellowstone. Ranchers whose cattle and sheep grazed near the park were worried that the wolves would not stay inside the park's borders. They feared that the wolves would kill cattle and sheep. The managers of the wolf project tried to set up rules for handling wolves that killed farm animals, but many ranchers were still concerned.

Other people who were against the reintroduction of the wolves believed that it should be allowed to happen naturally. They thought that lone wolves that occasionally made their way south from Canada should be allowed to move into the park on their own and start packs. It might take many decades, but wolves would return to Yellowstone eventually.

A hungry wolf

Forming Your Own Opinion

Returning wolves to Yellowstone has caused controversy. Both sides have strong opinions and good points to make. Most people form **opinions** according to their values. Values are the things you think are important. What are your values? How do they affect your opinion about the reintroduction of the wolves to Yellowstone? The first paragraph of this article makes you want to root for the wolves. But what if it had described a hard-working rancher finding a valuable calf that had been killed by wolves? It's important to try to see both sides of a question and then decide for yourself.

opinions
(uh•**pin**•yuhns)—
decisions about which
side is right in an
argument or controversy

Opinions About Returning Wolves to Yellowstone National Park

For	Against
It will keep the elk at healthy numbers and protect the plant life. It improves the biodiversity (the number of different species in an area). It returns Yellowstone to the way it was 150 years ago. It returns wolves to the United States much earlier than they would return on their own. It allows visitors to the park to have experiences with wolves.	Farm animals will be killed. Reintroduction doesn't let nature (or the wolves) take its own course. Other ways to control the number of elk are just as good as reintroducing wolves. The wolves will not stay inside the boundaries of the park. If the reintroduction doesn't work, the wolves will be killed or put in zoos.

Put Your Habits to Work in

Literature | **Social Studies** | **Science** | **Math**

Before I Read Habit:
Check it out!

Skim the charts or graphs to see what the selection is about. This will help you know what to expect as you read it.

While I Read Habit:
Stop and ask, "Does it make sense?"

As you go along, stop every now and then to think about whether what you're reading fits with what you know about the topic.

After I Read Habit:
Use what I've read.

Identify the most important ideas and think about how you might use that information.

I thought the most interesting thing . . .

You may wish to use the **Put Your Habits to Work Sheet** on page 11 in your *Strategy Practice Book* to practice these habits in your other reading.

Unit 2
Lost Worlds
Theme: Mystery

In this unit, you will develop these 3 habits for all readers.

Before I Read Habit:
Decide what I need to know.

While I Read Habit:
Stop and ask, "If it doesn't make sense, what can I do?"

After I Read Habit:
React to what I've read.

Learn 3 of the 9 Habits

In this unit, you will work on three habits—one for before you read, one for while you are reading, and one for after you finish reading. Start with **Before I Read**. Read the habit and strategy. Then read my notes below.

Before I Read

Which **HABIT** will I learn?
Decide what I need to know.
If I develop this habit, I will have a reason for reading. I will understand it better and remember more of what I read.

Which **STRATEGY** will I use to learn this habit?
Use the headings to ask purpose-setting questions.

My Notes

- Strategy says to look at the headings and use them to ask purpose-setting questions.

- That means I need to turn these into questions so I will have some idea of what I will read about and why.

- After looking at the headings, I decided that there are 3 things I want to know. What is Machu Picchu? Why was it lost? How was it found?

The Someday That Never Came:

Machu Picchu

The train climbed higher and higher, round and round, straight up! All the way from **Cuzco**, many miles back, the road had gotten steeper and steeper. Rachelle and her family were high up in the Andes [**an**•deez] Mountains on their way to **Machu Picchu**. Rachelle looked out one side of the train, then the other, and up ahead as best she could. But it only looked to her as if they were going up the steepest mountain she had ever seen! It looked as if they were on a train to the clouds, not on a train to an Inca city built hundreds of years ago.

Rachelle pulled on her dad's sleeve. "Dad, are you sure we're on the right train?" she asked. "It looks as if this train is going nowhere!"

"Don't worry, Rachelle. We're on the right train. We have many more hours to travel, though. This is because even after we leave the train, we still have a long bus ride." Her dad peered out of the train window, too. "It's just that Machu Picchu is a very hard place to get to. That's why no one found it for so long." He went on to tell Rachelle about the mystery of Machu Picchu.

Cuzco (**koo**•skoh)—a city in Peru

Machu Picchu (**mahch**•oo **peek**•choo)— an ancient city built by the Inca

Train station for the train from Cusco, Peru, to Machu Picchu

Now read the habit and strategy for **While I Read**. When you see ❓, read my notes in the margin.

While I Read

Which **HABIT** will I learn?
Stop and ask, "If it doesn't make sense, what can I do?"
If I develop this habit, I will stop and figure out what to do so what I'm reading makes sense. Then I can keep reading and not be lost.

Which **STRATEGY** will I use to learn this habit?
Use context clues to help me understand the meanings of unknown words.

Stop and Ask ❓

If it doesn't make sense, what can I do? Use context clues to help me understand the meanings of unknown words.

I wasn't sure what the word *empire* meant, so I reread the sentence and read around the word and decided that it probably meant that it was a very powerful country that ruled a large area.

What Was Machu Picchu Like?

Back in the 1400s, one of the groups of people who lived in Peru was called the Inca [**ing**·kuh]. By the 1400s, they ruled much of South America west of the Andes Mountains. These mountains rise steeply along the west coast of South America. The Inca built stone roads all through them. The roads were very important to their empire. They helped the Inca send messengers quickly to all parts of their empire. These stone roads helped them move important trade goods, like food, cloth, and gold, from one place to another pretty easily. These roads also helped the Inca army move quickly. That was important for two reasons. One, it helped keep the empire strong. And two, it helped the rulers make sure their people were taken care of and safe. ❓ *Strategy Alert!*

The rulers took a part of everything that was made by the people, grown by the people, and taken out of the ground by the people—namely, tons of gold and emeralds. In return, the rulers made sure the people were taken care of and safe. The Inca rulers were pagan religious leaders, too, and part of their job was to make sure that their gods were kept happy.  *Strategy Alert!*

The rulers also asked the people to spend some time each year working on public projects such as buildings and roads. The main road was built so well that many parts of it, now called the Inca Trail, are still used today. When the distance between towns was long, the Inca built inns and resting places, just like roadside rest stops along the highways in the U.S. The Inca probably started to build Machu Picchu around the middle of the 1400s. Some people think it was built just as one of those resting places along the Inca Trail.

Machu Picchu was probably more of a city than a simple resting place along the road. The stone buildings were put together with great skill. The stones that were used to form the buildings do not all have square corners. In fact, one stone was carefully carved with 37 angles to align perfectly as a corner with many other stones. The question is, "Would that much art, effort, and skill be put into a roadside rest stop?" In addition, several large homes, or palaces, are found at Machu Picchu. This leads some people to think that the city may have been a vacation spot for wealthy Inca people. *Strategy Alert!*

The ruins of Machu Picchu

Stop and Ask

If it doesn't make sense, what can I do? Use context clues to help me understand the meanings of unknown words.

I wasn't sure what the word *pagan* meant, so I read around the word and decided it had something to do with the Inca's kind of gods.

Stop and Ask

If it doesn't make sense, what can I do? Use context clues to help me understand the meanings of unknown words.

I wasn't sure what the word *align* meant, so I read around the word and decided it meant "fit" because that would make sense with the word "perfectly."

An unusual building with three large windows was built along one side of the city. No other Inca building in all of Peru has three windows or windows that large. This building may have been used to check the position of the sun in the sky. This leads some people to think Machu Picchu might have been built as a special place to hold religious ceremonies.

Machu Picchu: Lost

We believe that people lived in Machu Picchu until the early 1500s. When Spanish invaders conquered the Incas in the middle 1500s, the city was already deserted. No one knows why the city was built, and no one knows why it was deserted. It may have been too hard to get up to, perched high in the Andes between two mountain peaks. Some scientists think the water ran out. The water in Machu Picchu was supplied from underground springs. Maybe they dried up. ? *Strategy Alert!*

Machu Picchu ruins and Huayna Picchu Mountain

Whatever the reason, Machu Picchu was deserted many years ago. It's strange, but this desertion is what saved the city in the long run. The Spanish army destroyed the Inca empire. They killed many people and took away the riches. But the Spanish army never found Machu Picchu, high in the misty Andes Mountains. Through Machu Picchu's wonderful buildings with windows and doorways, we get a glimpse, just a glimpse, of this once-thriving culture and its skills in art and building. ? *Strategy Alert!*

Stop and Ask ?

If it doesn't make sense, what can I do? Use context clues to help me understand the meanings of unknown words.

● ● ● ● ● ● ● ● ● ● ●

I wasn't sure what the word *perched* meant, so I read around the word again and I decided it meant "sat" because that would make sense in the sentence.

Stop and Ask ?

If it doesn't make sense, what can I do? Use context clues to help me understand the meanings of unknown words.

● ● ● ● ● ● ● ● ● ● ●

I wasn't sure what the word *glimpse* meant. I read around the word and decided that it meant a quick look.

Machu Picchu: Found

For hundreds of years, Machu Picchu sat empty. Trees took root in the wide **plazas**. Roofs thatched with grass caved in. Birds nested in the **niches** in the massive stone walls. If you didn't know where to look, you would never know it was there. By the early 1900s, only a few people living high in the Andes still knew about the lost city. That's when Hiram Bingham arrived. Bingham was a history teacher from Yale. He was looking for the lost Inca city of Vilcabamba [vil•kuh•**bahm**•buh]. Based on papers written by Spanish people in the 1500s, Bingham thought the city would be somewhere northwest of Cuzco. In 1911, with the help of a local guide, he found Machu Picchu instead. **?** *Strategy Alert!*

The trail to Machu Picchu zigzagged back and forth, back and forth. Had it gone straight up, it would have been very dangerous. At one point, Bingham and his group had to cross a narrow rope bridge that swayed over a deep canyon. Bingham's group realized they would have to build better bridges and roads before they could really explore Machu Picchu. Otherwise, they would not be able to bring the equipment and gear they needed up to the city.

Part of the Inca Trail in Cuzco, Peru

plazas (**plah**•zuhz)—public squares

niches (**nich**•uhz)—ledges cut into walls where statues can be displayed

Stop and Ask **?**

If it doesn't make sense, what can I do? Use context clues to help me understand the meanings of unknown words.

I wasn't sure what the word *thatched* meant. I read around the word and saw that it had something to do with roofs with grass. I decided that this meant the roofs were made of grass.

Stop and Ask ❓

If it doesn't make sense, what can I do? Use context clues to help me understand the meanings of unknown words.

· · · · · · · · · · · ·

I wasn't sure what the word excavated meant so I read around the word and saw that it said they removed dirt and debris. I think that's what excavated means.

llamas (lah·muhz)— South American animals used to carry things

Stop and Ask ❓

If it doesn't make sense, what can I do? Use context clues to help me understand the meanings of unknown words.

· · · · · · · · · · ·

I wasn't sure what bustling meant so I read around the word. It seems to go with "city," "noisy," and "activity." I think it means "busy."

Over the next several years, Bingham led teams that excavated the city. (He led teams that found Vilcabamba, too.) They removed dirt, rock, and plants that had covered the stone. They returned toppled stones to the tops of walls. They made drawings and took photographs and published them in *National Geographic*. Now everyone could see the fountains, stairways, and terraces of Machu Picchu. Everyone could see how its plazas, palaces, and temples were laid out. Today, Machu Picchu is the most popular tourist attraction in Peru. ❓ *Strategy Alert!*

The terraces of Machu Picchu

Machu Picchu: Mystery

"Dad, what's that path with the backpackers on it?" Rachelle pointed out the window.

"That's the old Inca Trail," he answered. "It takes backpackers 5 or 6 days to reach Machu Picchu on it." Her dad's voice got softer. "Imagine climbing the Inca Trail 500 years ago, a dozen **llamas** trailing out behind you. You're carrying corn or maybe expensive weavings for an Inca prince. The city is noisy and bustling with activity when you arrive." His voice got softer still. "Then imagine that you are the last one to leave. Imagine leaving the empty, silent city behind, moving lower and lower on the mountain until the city is lost in the mist . . ."

"Yes." Rachelle picked up the story. "Maybe you hoped you'd be back someday—a someday that never came." ❓ *Strategy Alert!*

Now read the habit and strategy for **After I Read**. Then read my notes below.

After I Read

Which **HABIT** will I learn?
React to what I've read.
If I develop this habit, I will take time to think about what I've just read. Deciding what I think and what I feel helps me remember it better.

Which **STRATEGY** will I use to learn this habit?
Create a graphic organizer of what I've read.

My Notes

- The strategy says to create a graphic organizer.
- I'll make a table of what I've read.
- I'll use the headings in the selection as headings in my table.
- Then I can fill in the table with information from the selection.

Now it's time to practice the three habits and strategies you learned when you read "The Someday That Never Came: Machu Picchu." Reread the habit and strategy below and then do it!

Before I Read

Which **HABIT** will I practice?
Decide what I need to know.
If I develop this habit, I will have a reason for reading. I will understand it better and remember more of what I read.

Which **STRATEGY** will I use to practice this habit?
Use the headings to ask purpose-setting questions.

Use the **Before I Read Strategy Sheet** for "The Mystery of Great Zimbabwe" on page 12 in the *Strategy Practice Book* to help you decide what you need to know.

The Mystery of Great Zimbabwe

As soon as the car stopped, Tony climbed out of the back seat. It had been a long drive to **Great Zimbabwe** from **Harare** and he was eager to look around. The sky was brilliant blue. All around, low trees grew in clumps of deep green in the yellow-gold grasses.

The landscape was beautiful, but it wasn't what captured Tony's attention. Right in front of Tony rose a huge white stone wall. It stood out brightly against the wide, open space he and his parents had driven through.

"Wow!" Tony said. "Mom, this is a lot bigger than I thought it would be."

Tony's mom smiled. "Go ahead and explore, Tony, but be careful." She ran her hand over Tony's hair. "I'm going inside with the tour. Your dad will stay with you."

Great Zimbabwe
(grayt zim•**bahb**•way)
—a very old city in the country of Zimbabwe

Harare (huh•**rah**•ray)
—the capital city of Zimbabwe

The Great Enclosure

Remember the *Strategy Alerts!* in **While I Read** in the last selection? They reminded you to use context clues to help you understand the meanings of unknown words. Now do the same thing with this selection.

While I Read

Which **HABIT** will I practice?

Stop and ask, "If it doesn't make sense, what can I do?"

If I develop this habit, I will stop and figure out what to do so what I'm reading makes sense. Then I can keep reading and not be lost.

Which **STRATEGY** will I use to practice this habit?

Use context clues to help me understand the meanings of unknown words.

Use the **While I Read Strategy Sheet** for "The Mystery of Great Zimbabwe" on page 13 in the *Strategy Practice Book* as you read.

granite (**gran**·it)—a very hard stone used for building

enclosures (in·**kloh**·zhurz)—spaces surrounded (closed in) by a fence or walls

Stop and Ask ?

If it doesn't make sense, what can I do? Use context clues to help me understand the meanings of unknown words.

Great Zimbabwe is what remains of the capital city of a great kingdom that ruled southeast Africa from about 1200 until about 1450. All that's left now is the strongest parts of what was built. These strongest parts are great **granite** walls that enclose two main areas and piles of stone that show where other **enclosures** used to be.

The Great Enclosure

"This is the Great Enclosure we talked about in the car, Tony," his dad said. "Do you remember what the guidebook said about how the walls were built?"

Tony ran his hand over the wall. "I can see now what the book meant." He traced the line between two stones with his finger. "The stones fit together exactly without any mortar to stick them together." Tony peered closer. "It's so tight I can't even get my fingernail between these two stones." *Strategy Alert!*

Tony looked up. The stone wall towered over him. That made him think of the tower. "Let's go inside the walls, Dad. I want to see the tower."

The Tower

Tony and his dad went through an opening in the thick double walls into a large oval-shaped area. Sections of walls were broken down and there were piles of rubble. When the Great Enclosure was first built, there were walls inside. The walls separated the space into different areas. At one end was a platform and a round tower that had no doors and no windows.  *Strategy Alert!*

"You can't go in. You can't get out. Dad, what was that tower used for?" Tony asked.

"No one knows, Tony," his dad answered. "It's about 34 feet tall—about two feet taller than the walls. Most scientists who have studied Great Zimbabwe think it was a symbol for something."

"So it wasn't used for storing grain or as a lookout tower?" Tony asked.

"No," his dad said. "It may have stood for the strength of the people or the strength of the rulers. It may have been a symbol for having plenty of food. This enclosure was probably where the rulers lived. They built houses of clay with roofs made of grass and then built the walls around the houses. The houses have mostly broken down, though. Clay doesn't last as long as stone."  *Strategy Alert!*

The tower of Great Zimbabwe

Stop and Ask ?

If it doesn't make sense, what can I do? Use context clues to help me understand the meanings of unknown words.

Stop and Ask ?

If it doesn't make sense, what can I do? Use context clues to help me understand the meanings of unknown words.

obtained (ob·taynd)—
got

fortress (for·truhs)—
fort; a place of safety or
protection

Stop and Ask ?

If it doesn't make
sense, what can I
do? Use context
clues to help me
understand the
meanings of
unknown words.

Stop and Ask ?

If it doesn't make
sense, what can I
do? Use context
clues to help me
understand the
meanings of
unknown words.

Cooking the Stone

"Look, there's Mom." Tony and his dad walked over to where Tony's mom was listening to a guide.

"It is interesting how the builders **obtained** the stone," the guide was saying. "All around here are places where rocks stick up above the soil. And I mean BIG rocks. If you look up, you will see the Hill **Fortress**, high above us." He gestured to another rock formation on a hill about half a mile away. "You'll see that the whole hill the ruins are sitting on is one piece of granite!"

? *Strategy Alert!*

Tony was impatient. "Excuse me, sir, but what does that have to do with getting the stone for the walls?"

"The builders would build a fire on top of or around a giant hunk of granite until the rock got very hot," the guide explained.

Rock formation at Great Zimbabwe National Monument

"Then they poured cold, cold water on the hot rock. The change in temperature caused the rock to crack into flat slabs, almost like bricks. In a way, the Zimbabwe builders cooked the stone!"

"Cool!" Tony said. "So no one had to make bricks one by one or dig rock out of the ground."

"That's right," said the guide. "But the building of the Great Enclosure, the Hill Fortress, and the many other enclosures that are gone now still took a very large amount of skill. No European cultures at that time could build such fine walls without mortar. The wall also shows that the culture was successful enough for people to take time away from meeting their daily needs for food and shelter and work on this project." The guide looked at his watch. "Take a few more minutes here and then we'll take the trail up to the Hill Fortress." ? *Strategy Alert!*

The ruins of Great Zimbabwe overlooking the lush land of Zimbabwe, Africa

The Hill Fortress

Of course, Tony couldn't wait. He spotted the trail and reached the Hill Fortress well before the tour group. His dad was right behind him. The Hill Fortress looked different. It was older and not as even as the Great Enclosure. In many places, parts of the granite hill stuck out of the ground and stones were fitted around the natural rock to make the wall. Tony and his dad explored three areas that looked as if they used to be walled off.

When the tour group came up, the guide was talking about the history of the African people who built Great Zimbabwe. "Early Shona [**shoh**·nuh] people settled in this area of Africa more than a thousand years ago. It's a high area, and the rainfall was good. The people herded cattle, so they needed the grass to grow well. The abundant rain helped this growth. Gradually, they developed trading routes with cities on the east coast of Africa. Beads and pottery and other items found here came from India, China, and African coastal areas. The Shona people traded iron and gold for these items. Controlling the trade routes brought wealth to the people. They had time to develop government and a ruling class. The Hill Fortress and the Great Enclosure were built between 1250 and 1400." ❓ *Strategy Alert!*

Stop and Ask

If it doesn't make sense, what can I do? Use context clues to help me understand the meanings of unknown words.

Tony interrupted. "It's the ruling class that lived here in the fortress, right?"

"Yes," the guide answered. "The most important people probably lived up here in the fortress. Other rulers lived in the Great Enclosure. Some scientists think that the walls of the Great Enclosure were built just for show. The rulers wanted everyone to see how important they were!"

A Mystery to Solve

Tony interrupted again. "If they were so important, where are they now? What happened to the people who lived in Great Zimbabwe?"

"That, young friend, is the million-dollar question," the guide said. "By about 500 years ago, this great fortress and the enclosure in the valley below were deserted. No one really knows why this place was built and no one knows why it was **abandoned**. No one knows what the tower was for. It's a great mystery." He smiled at Tony. "Do you like to solve mysteries?"

"I sure do," Tony answered.

"Well, then, maybe the solution of this mystery is for you!"

abandoned
(uh•**ban**•duhnd)—left behind

Ruin of a stairway at Great Zimbabwe

Remember that you're not finished until you've reacted to what you've read.

After I Read

Which **HABIT** will I practice?
React to what I've read.
If I develop this habit, I will take time to think about what I've just read. Deciding what I think and what I feel helps me remember it better.

Which **STRATEGY** will I use to practice this habit?
Create a graphic organizer of what I've read.

Use the **After I Read Strategy Sheet** for "The Mystery of Great Zimbabwe" on page 14 in the *Strategy Practice Book* to help you react to what you've read.

Apply 3 of the 9 Habits

Now read "A Story of the Anasazi" and apply these three habits and strategies.

Before I Read

Which **HABIT** will I apply?
Decide what I need to know.

Which **STRATEGY** will I use to apply this habit?
Use the headings to ask purpose-setting questions.

While I Read

Which **HABIT** will I apply?
Stop and ask, "If it doesn't make sense, what can I do?"

Which **STRATEGY** will I use to apply this habit?
Use context clues to help me understand the meanings of unknown words.

After I Read

Which **HABIT** will I apply?
React to what I've read.

Which **STRATEGY** will I use to apply this habit?
Create a graphic organizer of what I've read.

 Use the **Self-Assessment Sheet** for "A Story of the Anasazi" on pages 15–16 in the *Strategy Practice Book* as you read to see how well you can apply the habits and strategies.

A Story of the Anasazi

About 2,000 years ago, a group of wanderers hunted animals and gathered food plants in the area we now call the American Southwest. In one area, they noticed that there were many food animals and the plants grew well. These areas, called **mesas,** were high, cut by narrow canyons. In some places, the walls of the canyons were worn away to make huge shallow caves in the rock. The wanderers took shelter in these caves and hunted and gathered on the mesas above. The weather was warm and dry. The people spent most of their time outdoors. These people are now known as the Anasazi [ahn•uh•**sahz**•ee].

mesas (**may**•suhz)— high, flat areas of land, like tabletops

Ancient dwellings in the American Southwest

The Pit House Time

By the year 700, the people were living in houses up on the mesas. Their houses were called pit houses. These Anasazi people made a certain kind of basket. When that type of basket is found, we know that those Anasazi lived in pit houses. The **remains** of the pit houses can be seen today. A pit with a flat bottom was dug in the earth. Wooden poles held up a roof of sticks and mud. There was a hole in the center of the roof where smoke could get out. That's also how the people got in and out of the house. They put a ladder in the hole. Scientists are able to tell how old the pit houses are by looking at the growth rings in the wooden poles. But no one knows why the people moved from the caves up to the mesas.

Tourist exploring a pit house ruin at Pecos National Monument, New Mexico

Early Pueblos

Gradually, the Anasazi built their homes more and more above ground. Eventually, they built rows of one-room homes that shared a wall, like a row of apartments. The buildings built this way—with square rooms that share walls with other rooms—are called pueblos [**pweb**·lohz]. Families probably lived together in the same row. The houses gradually came to be made of sandstone bricks instead of sticks and mud. By 1050, the people were living above the ground in houses that had two stories. The Anasazi who lived in pueblos made a certain kind of pottery. When that pottery is found, we know that those Anasazi lived during the time of the pueblos. They relied on farming for much of their food.

remains (ree·**maynz**)— what is left over

When the people moved aboveground, two things remained from the earlier time. First, they had to go up to go down. The first-floor rooms usually didn't have a door. People climbed up a ladder to the roof and then down another ladder to get inside. The second thing that stayed the same was the presence of a pit house. Now, however, the pit house became a community center instead of a home. Religious rituals and meetings were held there.

Ceremonial room, Great Kiva, Aztec Ruins National Park, New Mexico

Pit houses that served the community were called **kivas** [**kee**·vuhz]. Throughout the time the Anasazi lived as a distinct group of people, they had kivas. The kiva was round and eventually came to be made of brick. But it was always underground. Historians and scientists can only guess at the activities that took place in the kiva. No written records exist. Every kiva had a fireplace and a special hole in the ground called a sipapu [si·**pah**·poo]. The sipapu represented the place where living things had first come from the earth.

Later Pueblos

The Anasazi built many buildings in wide Chaco [**chahk**·oh] Canyon in northwest New Mexico. They probably started building there about a thousand years ago. As more people moved there, they added more and more rooms and stories to the buildings. One town, called Pueblo Bonito [boh·**nee**·toh], can be seen today. The town was made of one large building with 800 rooms and 37 kivas. The pueblos at Chaco Canyon are a mystery. No one knows why the Anasazi chose to build such large settlements there. Water was hard to get then and now, and the location doesn't seem to be close to any other important places. But at one time Pueblo Bonito must have been a very busy place. Imagine people climbing ladders into and out of the 800 rooms, smoke coming from openings in the roofs, and perhaps the sound of chanting coming from one of the kivas.

The Anasazi built with the sandstone that was all around them. Sandstone is a soft type of rock, often gold or golden brown. The Anasazi used stone and bone tools to loosen and shape their bricks. They had no metal, such as iron or copper. They held the bricks together with a thick mud mortar. They often put a layer of plaster over the surface of the bricks to make them look smooth.

Anasazi people had busy lives. They went to distant areas to trade. They developed a complex set of religious rituals. They developed great skill in building, pottery, and weaving. They even built roads. Miles and miles of wide, flat roads lead out in every direction from the Chaco Canyon pueblos.

Back to the Cliffs

For reasons no one knows, at about the same time they began building cities like Pueblo Bonito, the Anasazi began to return to the caves. They took their building methods with them. They carried thousands of their sandstone bricks up the faces of the cliffs, using ladders and toeholds. High up in the face of the cliff, they built huge, complex buildings in large caves. The buildings in the cliff were just as complex as the ones they built on the valley floor in Chaco Canyon. In some areas, wherever there is a cave of any size, there is a pueblo inside. It might be two rooms or it might be fifty rooms. A pueblo called Cliff Palace at Mesa Verde [**vair**·day] National Park is an example of a large cliff dwelling.

Sometime around 1100, the Anasazi population stopped growing. The people stopped building. By the year 1300, the beautiful buildings and busy towns were empty. What happened? There were lengthy droughts in the 1100s and the 1200s that might have led people to move to wetter places. There may have been fights among the rulers of different groups of the Anasazi, causing people to scatter. Or the reason may be something we have not yet imagined.

Ruins of cliff dwellings, Mesa Verde National Park, Colorado

The Riddle of the Anasazi

The Anasazi people moved away to live with other groups in the area. But the buildings were preserved by the very dryness that may have led to their being deserted. They and the people who built them came to public awareness in the late 1800s. It became a popular activity to go to Anasazi places to look for old pots, baskets, and other remains of these people. Several people set up business as tour guides, earning money for showing people where the most interesting places were. Archaeologists first excavated Anasazi sites in the first decade of the 1900s. Now many of the important places are under the protection of the National Park Service. The National Park Service makes sure that the Anasazi places are not damaged.

Many people have studied and thought about the Anasazi. They try to put the clues together to solve the riddles of this ancient American culture. Still, all that can be offered is a story of the Anasazi. There are many opinions, and many arguments, about how and why they lived and died, with no real explanation. The one voice missing is the voice of the Anasazi themselves. They speak only through the buildings, baskets, and pots they left behind. But listen closely. As the wind blows through the abandoned pueblos, maybe we can hear their voices.

Anasazi pottery

Pueblo Bonito, Chaco Canyon, New Mexico

Put Your Habits to Work in

Before I Read Habit:
Decide what I need to know.

Use the headings to ask purpose-setting questions. This will give you a reason for reading so you'll understand it better and remember more of what you read.

Earth, Like Bread

From where you are standing, get out a shovel and start digging. Dig straight down towards the center of Earth and don't stop until you have dug about 3,960 miles. When you're done, you will be at the very center of Earth, in the middle of an area called the inner core. Along the way, you'll have dug through the

While I Read Habit:
Stop and ask, "If it doesn't make sense, what can I do?"

Use context clues to help you understand the meanings of unknown words.

begins. The uppermost part of the atmosphere is the exosphere. Here Earth's atmosphere gradually changes into the void of space, sometimes called "outer space." Is this where space

The Earth, Dissected

After I Read Habit:
React to what I've read.

Make a graphic organizer about what you've read.

I made a . . .

You may wish to use the **Put Your Habits to Work Sheet** on page 17 in your *Strategy Practice Book* to practice these habits in your other reading.

Unit 3
Native American Games We Play
Theme: Sports

In this unit, you will develop these 3 habits for all readers.

Before I Read Habit:
Think about what I know about the subject.

While I Read Habit:
Stop and ask, "How does it connect to what I know?"

After I Read Habit:
Use what I've read.

In this unit, you will work on three habits—one for before you read, one for while you are reading, and one for after you finish reading. Start with **Before I Read**. Read the habit and strategy. Then read my notes below.

Before I Read

Which **HABIT** will I learn?

Think about what I know about the subject.

If I develop this habit, I will bring to mind what I already know about the subject. This gets me ready to connect what I read to what I know so I will understand it better.

Which **STRATEGY** will I use to learn this habit?

Use the headings to decide what I know about this topic.

My Notes

- Strategy says to use the headings to decide what I know about this topic.
- The headings are "The First Lacrosse Games," "Tamer Times," "Looking Back," and "Traditions Continue."
- It looks as though this selection is going to be about the history of lacrosse.
- I've seen lacrosse on TV, but I don't know much about it.
- Now I really want to read more to find out about this game.

A Love for Lacrosse

The game of lacrosse was given its name by a French **missionary**. However, the game was invented by Native Americans. Members of the Iroquois nation developed the **version** of lacrosse that is now played. Choctaw men also played—and still play—the game with great enthusiasm.

When Europeans were still new to North America, French settlers watched Native American teams play this game. The settlers put together their own teams so they could play each other. By 1867, lacrosse had become the national sport of Canada. Now it's played throughout the world.

Lacrosse is similar in some ways to ice hockey. However, lacrosse is played on grass, not ice, and with a ball instead of a puck. Lacrosse sticks are shaped differently, too, to allow players to scoop up the ball and throw it.

Making lacrosse sticks is an artform.

missionary (**mi**·shuh·ner·ee)—a person sent to another culture to introduce his or her religion to the native people of that culture

version (**vur**·zhuhn)— one of various ways of doing something

Now read the habit and strategy for **While I Read**. When you see ❓, read my notes in the margin.

While I Read

Which HABIT will I learn?

Stop and ask, "How does it connect to what I know?"

If I develop this habit, I will think about how what I'm reading fits with what I know. This helps me understand the new material and remember it better.

Which STRATEGY will I use to learn this habit?

Think about whether I've ever done something similar.

---

bishop (**bish**·uhp)—a high-ranking member of a church

warriors (**wawr**·ee·uhrz) —people who fight in wars

Stop and Ask ❓

How does this connect to what I know? Think about whether I've ever done something similar.

I have seen hockey played before and my friends and I have even played street hockey, so I can imagine what lacrosse must look like.

The First Lacrosse Games

When Native Americans played lacrosse long ago, the ball was made of stuffed deerskin. Like modern sticks, their sticks had a hoop at one end. Leather strips crisscrossed the hoop. The strips formed a pocket so players could catch or scoop up and throw the ball. The hoops used by different Native American groups were shaped slightly differently. Some groups used two sticks, one in each hand. Others used one.

To that French missionary long ago, the stick looked like a **bishop**'s cross, so he called the game "lacrosse." Two Native American names for the game are *tokonhon* [tah·**kohn**·huhn] and *ishtaboli* [ish·tah·**boh**·lee], both of which mean "little-brother-of-war." For Native Americans, one purpose of the game was to test the strength and courage of young **warriors**. ❓ *Strategy Alert!*

In games long ago, the playing field might be a different size for every game. Sometimes the field stretched for a mile across the meadow or prairie. Teams could have any number of players, as long as both sides were even. There might be hundreds of players spread across the field battling each other, trying to send the ball between their **opponents'** goal posts at the end of the field. In the 1830s, the artist George Catlin painted these large groups of players struggling with each other.

A game might last for days. During that time, players were stomped, trampled, tackled, and kicked. Some of them were seriously injured and even killed!  *Strategy Alert!*

"Ball Play of the Choctaw—Ball Up" painted by George Catlin

Tamer Times

Today, men's lacrosse is played on a field that measures 60 by 110 yards. The field for women's lacrosse is usually 70 by 120 yards. At each end are goals that look much like hockey nets. The ball is made of hard rubber. It is a little smaller than a tennis ball. Each player carries one stick, or crosse. The end of the stick splits apart, forming an opening that is filled with a net of leather strips or strong cord. The goalie carries a crosse with a wider net.

Stop and Ask ❓

How does this connect to what I know? Think about whether I've ever done something similar.

• • • • • • • • • •

This doesn't seem like any game I've ever seen. It seems a lot more dangerous than hockey games I've seen or played.

opposing (uh•**poh**•zing)
—on the other side

Men's teams have 10 players, while women's teams have 12. The object is to use the crosse to pass the ball. It goes from one team member to another until it is sent into the **opposing** team's goal. Players are not allowed to touch the ball with their hands.

The game is played for an hour, which is divided into four periods. To prevent injuries, players may wear helmets with face guards, shoulder and arm padding, and gloves. Their uniforms are similar to those worn by ice hockey players.

Box lacrosse is played in a smaller, enclosed area. Often it's played indoors. Teams have only six players and lots of body contact. Box lacrosse is popular in Canada and the United States and among Iroquois teams. **?** *Strategy Alert!*

Men's and women's lacrosse teams

Stop and Ask **?**

How does this connect to what I know? Think about whether I've ever done something similar.

● ● ● ● ● ● ● ● ● ● ●

This description really does make lacrosse seem like hockey. It also seems a bit like soccer, only with a stick. In both games, players are not allowed to touch the ball.

Iroquois National vs Oneonta State College

Looking Back

Lacrosse is an important part of the Iroquois tradition. Long ago, it was played not only to have fun, but also to settle disputes between groups. The Iroquois believed that playing lacrosse would help heal the sick and lift people's hearts. The game also prepared young men for battle and helped older warriors stay in shape.

In the 1800s, Native American lacrosse teams were banned from competing in **amateur** national or international games. Some of these teams had charged admission to their games, which was against the rules for amateur teams. They were trying to raise money so they could travel to other games. In 1987, the Iroquois National team was formed, and Native American teams were finally allowed to play in amateur competitions. Since then, the Iroquois team has challenged other teams in the World Games and other international competitions. ❓ *Strategy Alert!*

amateur
(**am•uh•tur**)—involving players who do not get paid for what they do

Stop and Ask ❓

How does this connect to what I know? Think about whether I've ever done something similar.

We sell tickets to our school games, and so does the high school, and we're still amateurs. I wonder why the Native American teams were not allowed to play.

Traditions Continue

At Iroquois cultural celebrations today, people can watch the dances, taste the food, and buy handmade items, including lacrosse sticks. Many of these events include a series of lacrosse games. Whether the Iroquois still live in the homes of their ancestors or in big cities, the game of lacrosse brings them together. It's a link to their past and an important part of their present.

A tradition that spans generations

Now read the habit and strategy for **After I Read**. Then read my notes below.

After I Read

Which **HABIT** will I learn?
Use what I've read.
If I develop this habit, I will think about how I can apply what I just read to my schoolwork and my life. This makes reading really useful.

Which **STRATEGY** will I use to learn this habit?
Decide what I thought was interesting.

My Notes

- Strategy says to decide what I thought was interesting.
- I thought it was interesting that lacrosse was invented by Native Americans and today is played all over the world.
- I also thought it was interesting that lacrosse was used by Native Americans to settle disputes and train for war, as well as for fun.
- It was interesting that the playing field might be a mile long and that hundreds of people would play.

Now it's time to practice the three habits and strategies you learned when you read "A Love for Lacrosse." Reread the habit and strategy below and then do it!

Before I Read

Which **HABIT** will I practice?
Think about what I know about the subject.
If I develop this habit, I will bring to mind what I already know about the subject. This gets me ready to connect what I read to what I know so I will understand it better.

Which **STRATEGY** will I use to practice this habit?
Use the headings to decide what I know about this topic.

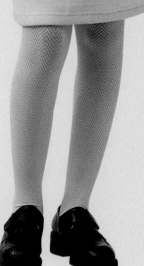

Use the **Before I Read Strategy Sheet** for "A Game 'Handed' Down" on page 18 in the *Strategy Practice Book* to help you think about what you know about this subject.

A Game "Handed" Down

Y ou have probably played the Hand Game without knowing who invented it. It's a guessing game. One player holds an object hidden in each hand. One of the objects has a special mark on it. Another player guesses which hand has the marked object.

Does that game sound familiar? The Spanish name for the Hand Game is *peón* [pay•**ohn**]. Native American names include *churchúrki* [choor•**choor**•kee] and *tinsok* [**tin**•sahk].

The Hand Game was probably first played by the Plains Indians. However, 81 different Native American groups have played this game. Most of them lived in the western two thirds of North America. In fact, many of these groups still have Hand Game teams that play

each other at tournaments. The Hand Game was and is a fun way for groups of warriors to try to outsmart each other. Groups can compete even if they speak different languages. They communicate with **gestures**.

gestures (**jes**•churz)— hand movements that communicate meaning

Remember the *Strategy Alerts!* in **While I Read** in the last selection? They reminded you to think about whether you've ever done something similar. Now do the same thing with this selection.

While I Read

Which **HABIT** will I practice?

Stop and ask, "How does it connect to what I know?"

If I develop this habit, I will think about how what I'm reading fits with what I know. This helps me understand the new material and remember it better.

Which **STRATEGY** will I use to practice this habit?

Think about whether I've ever done something similar.

Use the **While I Read Strategy Sheet** for "A Game 'Handed' Down" on page 19 in the *Strategy Practice Book* as you read.

The Rules of the Game

The Hand Game can be played by two people. It can also be played by two teams with the same number of players. When teams play, the players stand or sit in rows about 6 feet apart. Players from each side take turns hiding the marked object and guessing its location. Long ago, the objects were often small animal bones, one plain and one painted. Some pairs of bones were hollow, while some were solid. Sometimes one bone was marked by tying a leather strip around it. These bones were considered good luck for whoever owned them. They were passed from one **generation** to the next.

generation
(jen·uh·**ray**·shuhn)—
each part of a family, such as all the brothers and sisters or all the grandparents

If a player correctly guesses the location of the marked object, the person or team gets a wooden counting stick. Anyone making an incorrect guess loses a stick. When one player wins all the sticks, the game ends. The winner may get a prize. Sometimes an umpire makes sure everyone plays fairly. **?** *Strategy Alert!*

Stop and Ask ?

How does this connect to what I know? Think about whether I've ever done something similar.

Some sets of counting sticks are elaborately carved or painted. Some of them are sharpened to a point on one end, so they can be stuck into the ground between the two teams or players. Long ago, each stick sometimes represented a horse. Players won and lost horses as they played.

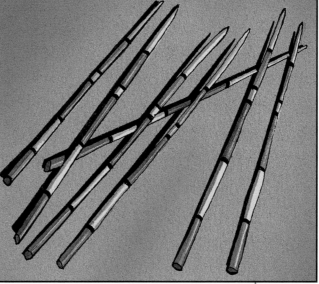

The Tricks of the Game

During the game, the player hiding the object often makes many hand movements to confuse the guesser. For example, one player might hold his hands above his head or behind his back. Another player might hide her hand movements under a blanket on her lap. The player or team usually sings while hiding the object, and someone plays a drum. The fast beat of the drum makes the game more exciting and helps confuse the guesser.

In some Native American groups long ago, only men were allowed to play the Hand Game. The women cheered them on and sang. In other groups, teams of women could play each other. Today women and men both play, but the drummer is usually still a man.

People watching these games often place bets on who is going to win. A game might last all day and all night. A winning team might become not only famous but also rich.

Today, teams have colors, jackets, songs, and many supporters. Every year, 31 tribal colleges and universities meet to hold different kinds of competitions. You can be sure they play the Hand Game.

 *Strategy Alert!*

Stop and Ask ?

How does this connect to what I know? Think about whether I've ever done something similar.

Try Your Hand!

You and a friend can play the Hand Game. First, you must find two objects the same size, small enough to be hidden in your hand. Mark one of them. For example, you might gather two stones and put a red spot on one with a marker. Make sure the objects are the same size. If one object is bigger than the other, the guesser will know which fist holds it.

Hand Game for Two Players

The first player will pick up the two objects and put both hands behind his or her back. When this player shows his or her hands again, the guesser must point to the hand with the marked object. If the guesser is correct, he or she gets a point. Players take turns hiding the objects and guessing the location of the marked one.

Hand Game for Teams

The teams sit facing each other. Both teams should have the same number of players. The teams can play the same way as described previously, with members of each team taking turns hiding and guessing.

In another version, the teams can play this way: The first player on one team will hide both objects in his or her hands. Then this player will pass one object to the next player on his or her team. The opposing team must guess whether the first player passed the marked object or kept it. If the team guesses correctly, it gets both objects and earns a point. Then the first player on the other team hides the objects and passes one on to a teammate.

If someone asks how you learned this game, say, "Native Americans taught me!" **?** *Strategy Alert!*

Stop and Ask ?

How does this connect to what I know? Think about whether I've ever done something similar.

Remember that you're not finished until you've used what you've read. Read the habit and strategy for **After I Read**.

After I Read

Which **HABIT** will I practice?
Use what I've read.
If I develop this habit, I will think about how I can apply what I just read to my schoolwork and my life. This makes reading really useful.

Which **STRATEGY** will I use to practice this habit?
Decide what I thought was interesting.

 Use the **After I Read Strategy Sheet** for "A Game 'Handed' Down" on page 20 in the *Strategy Practice Book* to help you use what you've read.

Apply 3 of the 9 Habits

Now read "A New/Old Way to Play Catch" and apply these three habits and strategies.

Before I Read

Which **HABIT** will I apply?
Think about what I know about the subject.

Which **STRATEGY** will I use to apply this habit?
Use the headings to decide what I know about this topic.

While I Read

Which **HABIT** will I apply?
Stop and ask, "How does it connect to what I know?"

Which **STRATEGY** will I use to apply this habit?
Think about whether I've ever done something similar.

After I Read

Which **HABIT** will I apply?
Use what I've read.

Which **STRATEGY** will I use to apply this habit?
Decide what I thought was interesting.

 Use the **Self-Assessment Sheet** for "A New/Old Way to Play Catch" on pages 21-22 in the *Strategy Practice Book* as you read to see how well you can apply the habits and strategies.

A New/Old Way to Play Catch

Have you ever tossed up a ring and tried to catch it on a stick? If you have, then you were playing a game invented long ago by Native Americans, who played many variations of this game. Together, these are called "toss and catch" or "ring and pin" games. Native Americans played these games for fun and for prizes.

Game Pieces From Nature

The pin was a thin, pointed piece of bone, antler, or wood. It might be 3 to 6 inches long. Some Native American groups eventually traded with the European settlers for iron needles, which they used in this game.

For the ring, players used whatever materials were available. For example, groups that lived on the Plains often used rings of dried buffalo skin. Groups in the Northwest used hollow deer-toe bones or salmon bones. Groups in the Southwest used dried squash **rinds**. People in the Northeast and Southeast wove rings of moose hair or grass. Instead of a ring, the Cree and other groups used a flat piece of leather with as many as 23 holes punched through it.

The pin was connected to the ring by a strong cord. The cord was just long enough to allow the tip of the pin to enter the ring. The player held the pin in one hand and swung the ring into the air. Then he or she tried to **spear** the ring with the pin before it fell. Sometimes leather, fur, or beads were attached to the ring to give it more weight. This extra weight pulled the ring down faster and made the game more difficult.

rinds (riendz)—skins of vegetables or fruits

spear (speer)—to strike with something pointed like a knife

In a more challenging variation of this game, three to nine rings were threaded onto a strong cord. These rings were often small, hollow bones, such as the toe bones of a deer. Some groups used the skulls of **rodents,** such as squirrels or rabbits. Each bone had as many as 10 holes punched in it. The player tried to catch the string of bones by sticking the needle through one of the holes. Loops of beads might be attached to the far ends of the rings to add more weight. The loops also kept the bones from slipping off the end of the cord.

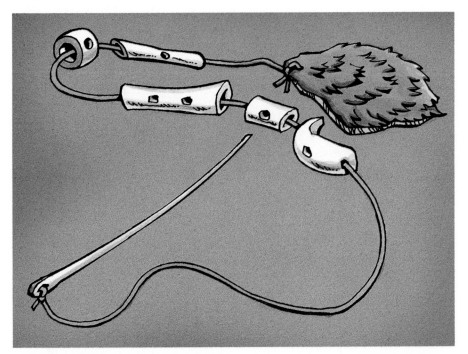

In some games, the string of bones ended with a piece of leather. Both the bones and the leather were **pierced** with holes.

Ring Rules

Everyone—men and women, boys and girls—played ring and pin games. One person could play alone to test his or her **coordination**. Often two players competed with each other. One player continued to toss and catch the ring until he or she missed. Then the other player took a turn. The more rings a player was able to catch, the more points he or she won. Different groups scored the bones differently. Some gave more points for bones that were closer to the pin. Some gave more points for bones that were farther from the pin.

rodents (**roh**•duhnts)— small gnawing mammals, such as rabbits and squirrels

pierced (peerst)— punctured

coordination (koh•or•dn•**ay**•shuhn)— ability to use one's body well to play games or do physical work

Sticking the pin through a hole in the side of a bone might be worth 5 points. Sticking the pin lengthwise through the same bone, which is more difficult, might be worth 25 points. Sticking the pin lengthwise through two bones might earn 50 points. Holes in different places on a leather target were usually worth different numbers of points. A game could continue until one player earned 100 points—or as much as 2,000 points.

Players often kept score by passing sticks back and forth. Each player might start out with 50 sticks, for example. When a player won points, he or she took sticks from the other player. When one player had won all the sticks, the game ended.

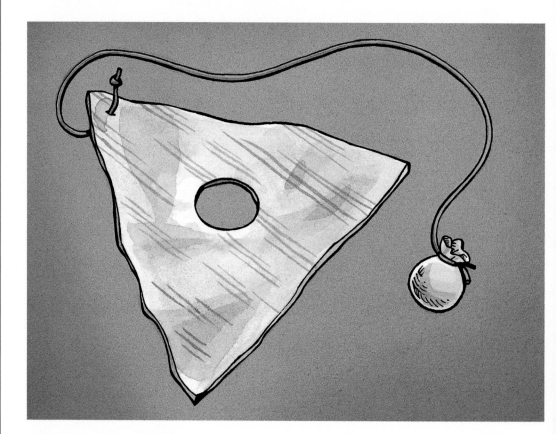

Try It Yourself

You can make a variation of this game and play it alone or with a friend. Children of the Penobscot [puh•**nahb**•skuht], who lived in Maine, often played a ball and triangle game. They made their triangles out of birch bark, but you can use a piece of heavy cardboard. You will also need a small rubber ball, 7" of string, scissors, a ruler, and tape.

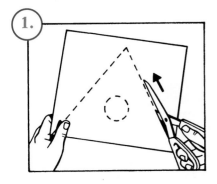

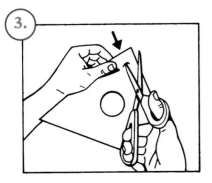

1. Cut a triangle out of the cardboard. Each side should be 6" long.

2. Carefully cut a hole in the center of the triangle. Make it a little bigger than the ball.

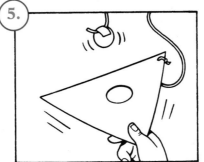

3. Use the scissors to punch a small hole in one corner of the triangle.

4. Tie one end of the string to the small hole. Firmly tape the other end of the string to the ball.

5. To play, hold the triangle by one of the corners without the string. Swing the ball up and try to make it fall through the hole.

Making Connections

The next time you are in a toy store, look for toys that are based on the "ring and pin" or the "toss and catch" game. See if any of the games say they were first played by Native Americans.

Put Your Habits to Work in

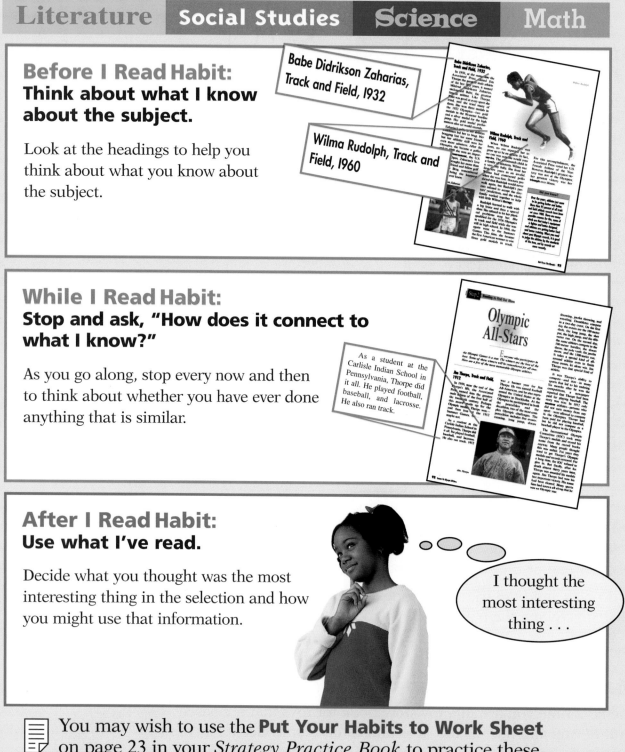

Before I Read Habit:
Think about what I know about the subject.

Look at the headings to help you think about what you know about the subject.

While I Read Habit:
Stop and ask, "How does it connect to what I know?"

As you go along, stop every now and then to think about whether you have ever done anything that is similar.

After I Read Habit:
Use what I've read.

Decide what you thought was the most interesting thing in the selection and how you might use that information.

I thought the most interesting thing . . .

You may wish to use the **Put Your Habits to Work Sheet** on page 23 in your *Strategy Practice Book* to practice these habits in your other reading.

Unit 4
American Tales
Theme: Classics

In this unit, you will develop these 3 habits for all readers.

Before I Read Habit:
Decide what I need to know.

While I Read Habit:
Stop and ask, "Does it make sense?"

After I Read Habit:
React to what I've read.

In this unit, you will work on three habits—one for before you read, one for while you are reading, and one for after you finish reading. Start with **Before I Read**. Read the habit and strategy. Then read my notes below.

Before I Read

Which **HABIT** will I learn?

Decide what I need to know.

If I develop this habit, I will have a reason for reading. I will understand it better and remember more of what I read.

Which **STRATEGY** will I use to learn this habit?

Use the genre to decide what might happen in the story.

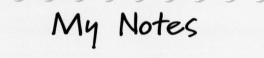

My Notes

- Strategy says to use what I know about the genre to decide what might happen in the story.
- I know a lot of American tales are tall tales, and Sally Ann's name makes me think of tall tales.
- A tall tale is funny and has characters that can do amazing things that other people can't do.
- I think Sally Ann Thunder Ann Whirlwind will do something amazing and funny, like other tall tale characters.

Sally Ann Thunder Ann Whirlwind

The hills and backwoods of Tennessee and Kentucky are full of stories. Some people say that stories float through the air like the feathery bits of dandelions and that you can just reach out and grab one whenever you need it. But some stories come through the air like high-pitched hollerin', demanding to be heard and told whether you think you need them or not. Stories about one very special character mostly fit in the last group.

One early spring day, Sally Ann Thunder Ann Whirlwind was walking through the woods when she heard a terrible **commotion**. A sound that was something like a coyote howlin' and something like a bobcat screechin' came flyin' through the trees.

"What in tarnation?" Sally Ann wondered, and she went to investigate. As the sound got louder, Sally Ann knew she was getting closer, but she still couldn't imagine what might be making that kind of racket. Then she saw it. It was a man, and with his head stuck in a tree, of all places.

commotion
(kuh·**moh**·shuhn)—a loud noise; hubbub

Now read the habit and strategy for **While I Read**. When you see ❓, read my notes in the margin.

While I Read

Which **HABIT** will I learn?

Stop and ask, "Does it make sense?"

If I develop this habit, I will stop now and then to make sure I understand what I'm reading.

Which **STRATEGY** will I use to learn this habit?

Decide if what's happening fits with the genre.

barge (bahrj)—a large flat boat used to carry goods along inland waterways

Stop and Ask ❓

Does it make sense? Decide if what's happening fits with the genre.

. . . .

It makes sense that Sally Ann says she can do all these impossible things like tote a river barge on her back. Characters in tall tales are always able to do things other people can't do.

"What's the matter, mister?" Sally Ann asked. The man eyed Sally Ann.

"My head's stuck, Sweetie. Could you go for help?" he said. Sally Ann looked down at the man.

"In the first place, don't call me Sweetie. In the second place, I am your help." Then Sally Ann took a handful of rattlesnakes out of her bag and began tying them together to make a long rope. "First off," she said, "Don't go thinkin' for a minute that I'm some delicate little flower. I can tote a river **barge** on my back, out-yell a screamin' panther, jump over my own shadow, and blow out the moonlight, if I get a mind to."

Sally Ann tied one end of her new rope to the branch that was holding the man. Then she stepped back several paces and began to pull on the rope. "And another thing," she said, "I can outride, out-rope, outrun, outswim, outclimb, and outlift any varmint around here." With that, she gave a final tug to the rope and plumb near pulled the tree apart. ❓ *Strategy Alert!*

The man's head was freed. He sat up and rubbed the back of his neck. When he could see straight again, he looked at Sally Ann. "What's your name?" he asked.

"Sally Ann Thunder Ann Whirlwind," she answered proudly. "If you behave yourself, you can call me Sally Ann. What's your name?"

"Davy Crockett," answered the stranger. And so began a beautiful friendship. Davy found himself more and more interested in this wild woman who'd saved his head. He went all over town asking about Sally Ann. He wanted to know everything. Well, all the town folk knew Sally Ann and they were all happy to tell the stories they knew. **?** *Strategy Alert!*

Stop and Ask **?**

Does it make sense? Decide if what's happening fits with the genre.

· · · · · · · · · · ·

It makes sense that Davy Crockett and Sally Ann would become friends. He is a hero of many American tales.

churning (**churn·**ing)
—using a long stick to beat cream in a crock called a churn for a long time until it thickens into butter

Stop and Ask ?

Does it make sense? Decide if what's happening fits with the genre.

· · · · · · · · · · · ·

It makes sense that Sally Ann would come up with a way to distract the bear, even if it couldn't really happen. In tall tales, characters have to be quick thinkers.

A favorite story was about how Sally Ann tamed a wild bear. One day, while she was **churning** butter, Sally Ann heard a scratching sound at her door. Before she could get up, the door swung open hard and the biggest, meanest bear she'd ever seen walked right in. The bear looked around Sally Ann's cabin, searching for the smoked hams he'd smelled from outside. Sally Ann was thinking fast. She picked up a bowl of dumplings and tossed one in the bear's mouth. The bear licked his chops in delight.

"OK," thought Sally Ann. "I can keep him busy with these dumplin's and lure him back outside." So, one by one, Sally Ann tossed the dumplings to the bear, all the time moving toward the door. There was just one problem. Sally Ann ran out of dumplings before she could get the bear outside. ? *Strategy Alert!*

With the dumplings gone, the bear started thinking that Sally Ann herself might be a nice lunch. He moved toward her. Sally Ann was backed into a corner with no way out that she could see. Then, just as the bear was about to grab her up, Sally Ann said, "Wouldn't you like to dance?"

The bear stopped. He LOVED dancing! Well, he forgot all about making a meal out of Sally Ann. Instead he smiled, bowed to her, and said, "I'd love to." So Sally Ann sang as she and the bear tromped and stomped across the floor. While they were dancing, Sally Ann managed to tie a piece of string around the bear's ankle and then to her churn. So while the bear kicked up his heels, he also finished churning Sally Ann's butter. ❓ *Strategy Alert!*

Stop and Ask ❓

Does it make sense? Decide if what's happening fits with the genre.

• • • • • • • • • • • • •

It makes sense that the bear would do something outrageous like churn butter while he danced. That's the sort of thing that happens in tall tales.

There were lots of other stories about Sally Ann. Some people said she could dance a rock to pieces. Some said they'd seen her ride a **panther** bareback. Others said she could laugh the bark off a tree. Davy Crockett listened to all the stories. Since the day Sally Ann had freed his head from that tree, Davy had been in love with her. Finally, one day he just couldn't stand it any longer. He put on his best coonskin cap and marched to Sally Ann's cabin. "Sally Ann, I want you to be my wife. Will you?" Davy asked.

"Well, my stars and possum dogs," Sally Ann said. "I can't think of any reason why not."

So Sally Ann and Davy were married. And they made quite a team. As a matter of fact, between the two of them there was nothing they couldn't do. Davy lived up to his reputation of being "King of the Wild Frontier." And Sally Ann lived up to her name of Sally Ann Thunder Ann Whirlwind, for she was always loud and never still.  *Strategy Alert!*

Stop and Ask ?

Does it make sense? Decide if what's happening fits with the genre.

· · · · · · · · · · ·

It makes sense that these two heroes would get married. Tall tales always have a happy ending.

Now read the habit and strategy for **After I Read**. Then read my notes below.

After I Read

Which **HABIT** will I learn?
React to what I've read.
If I develop this habit, I will take time to think about what I've just read. Deciding what I think and what I feel helps me remember it better.

Which **STRATEGY** will I use to learn this habit?
Decide whether I like the main character or not.

My Notes

- Strategy says to decide whether I like the main character.
- I think Sally Ann is pretty funny and very brave.
- Sally Ann is smart. She has a great imagination, especially when she feeds the bear dumplings and asks him to dance.

Now it's time to practice the three habits and strategies you learned when you read "Sally Ann Thunder Ann Whirlwind." Reread the habit and strategy below and then do it!

Before I Read

Which **HABIT** will I practice?
Decide what I need to know.
If I develop this habit, I will have a reason for reading. I will understand it better and remember more of what I read.

Which **STRATEGY** will I use to practice this habit?
Use the genre to decide what might happen in the story.

 Use the **Before I Read Strategy Sheet** for "Paul Bunyan" on page 24 in the *Strategy Practice Book* to help you decide what you need to know.

PAUL BUNYAN

Back in the olden days, an amazing baby was born in Maine. His name was Paul Bunyan. When he was only two weeks old, Paul weighed more than 100 pounds. For breakfast each morning, he ate 5 dozen eggs, 20 pounds of potatoes, and half a barrel of mush. He was big, but sweet-natured. And he wasn't much trouble until he got to be about nine months old. That's when he started to crawl, and since he weighed more than 500 pounds, he caused an earthquake every time he moved.

While I Read

Which **HABIT** will I practice?
Stop and ask, "Does it make sense?"
If I develop this habit, I will stop now and then to make sure I understand what I'm reading.

Which **STRATEGY** will I use to practice this habit?
Decide if what's happening fits with the genre.

Use the **While I Read Strategy Sheet** for "Paul Bunyan" on page 25 in the *Strategy Practice Book* as you read.

flints—hard rocks that cause sparks when two pieces are struck together

Does it make sense? Decide if what's happening fits with the genre.

The neighbors were not happy. They couldn't keep replacing things that shook off their shelves and broke. The constant rumbling and shaking made everyone nervous and grouchy. Finally they said that the baby had to go.

So Paul's parents took him to a cave in the woods far away from town. His mother cried when she said good-bye. His father gave him an ax, a knife, a fishing pole, and some **flints**. Then he said good-bye and good luck.

Paul cried for 30 days and nights. He cried a whole river of tears. Then one day he heard a flop, flop, flop. When he dried his eyes and looked around, he saw fish jumping in his river of tears. Soon he was catching trout with his fishing pole. He used his knife to clean the fish. He used his ax to cut wood for a fire. And he used his flints to start the fire. As he sat down to his big fish dinner, Paul smiled for the first time since he'd been in that cave. ❓ *Strategy Alert!*

Several years later, Paul was still living in that same cave. The winter wind that year was even colder than usual, whistling and howling and blowing snow in 20-foot drifts. Paul sat in his cave, watching the wild weather outside. Then a strange sound found its way to him. It sounded almost like a baby crying. Paul jumped up and ran outside. When the crying started again, he followed the sound.

He trudged through snow deep enough to bury normal-sized men. This worried him greatly. How could a baby survive this kind of storm? He had to find the little thing. Then, through the blinding snow, he noticed something blue sticking out of a tall snowbank. "What in the world!?" he said out loud. "It looks like a tail!" Paul grabbed hold and pulled. Out popped the biggest, bluest baby ox he had ever seen. The poor thing must've been awfully cold to have turned blue like that. Well, Paul reckoned that seein's how he didn't have another friend in the world and that baby ox didn't either, they'd make a good team. So, he named his new friend Babe and back they went to Paul's cave.  *Strategy Alert!*

Stop and Ask ?

Does it make sense? Decide if what's happening fits with the genre.

Turned out, Babe never did turn back to any kind of regular ox color, but stayed just as blue as the day Paul found him. Babe did grow so fast, though, that Paul could hardly believe it. Sometimes Paul would close his eyes and count to ten. Then when he opened his eyes again, he'd measure Babe to see how much the ox had grown while he wasn't looking. More than once, Babe grew a whole foot taller just in the count of ten. After a while, the cave seemed to be getting smaller and smaller. Paul looked at himself and at Babe. They were both so big and so powerful! Paul thought they should be doing something. So he invented **logging**.

Paul and Babe cut their way across the continent. They cut pine, spruce, and red willow in Michigan, Wisconsin, and Minnesota. In Kansas, they cut the cottonwoods so the farmers could plant wheat. In Iowa, they cut the oak trees so the farmers could plant corn.

Not long afterward, the two friends were seen traveling through Arizona. Paul walked along dragging his pick ax behind him. He didn't know until much later that he had accidentally carved a huge ditch. Today we call that ditch the Grand Canyon. **?** *Strategy Alert!*

logging (**lawg**·ing)— cutting down trees for lumber

Does it make sense? Decide if what's happening fits with the genre.

After some time had passed, Paul realized that he was tired. "I've been working all these years, Babe," he said to his friend. "Maybe it's time for me to let somebody else work. I think we should start a logging camp." So Babe and Paul went to Minnesota and put an ad in the paper:

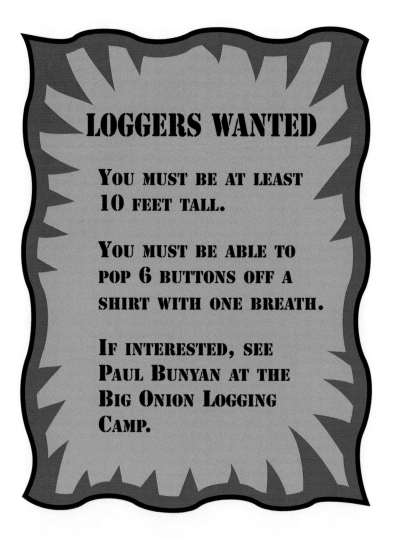

LOGGERS WANTED

YOU MUST BE AT LEAST 10 FEET TALL.

YOU MUST BE ABLE TO POP 6 BUTTONS OFF A SHIRT WITH ONE BREATH.

IF INTERESTED, SEE PAUL BUNYAN AT THE BIG ONION LOGGING CAMP.

Word spread fast. About 1,000 lumberjacks met all the requirements, and Paul hired them all. Of course, they needed a place to eat and sleep, so Paul built gigantic bunkhouses. Each bunkhouse was a mile long and tall enough for the bunk beds to be stacked 10 high. The chow table was so long that it took a whole week to pass the salt and pepper from one end to the other. Water for drinking and bathing came from several ponds that Paul and Babe dug. Today we call those ponds the Great Lakes. *Strategy Alert!*

Stop and Ask

Does it make sense? Decide if what's happening fits with the genre.

sawmill (**saw**·mil)—a place where logs are cut into lumber

Stop and Ask ?

Does it make sense? Decide if what's happening fits with the genre.

Paul took good care of his workers, and they worked hard. They cut trees so quickly that they couldn't carry all the logs to the **sawmill** fast enough. Logs started piling up all over Minnesota. Then Paul had an idea. "We'll float these logs down the river. When they reach the mill, we'll pull them out." So they threw all the piled-up logs into the river.

"The river's too crooked. Our logs are jamming up at the curves," said Paul. "Let's see what we can do about that." Then Paul tied one end of a rope around the end of the river and the other end to Babe's harness. "Pull, Babe, pull!" hollered Paul. Babe pulled. As a matter of fact, he pulled until all the bends and curves were straightened out. Then he and Paul stood on the bank and watched their logs float on toward the Big Onion. ? *Strategy Alert!*

Paul and his lumberjacks spent the next many years logging trees in Minnesota, then Washington, Oregon, and even Alaska. Eventually, Paul let his foreman take over the business. The last time anyone saw Paul, he was with Babe, of course, and the two of them were vacationing around the Arctic Circle.

> Remember that you're not finished until you've reacted to what you've read.

After I Read

Which **HABIT** will I practice?
React to what I've read.

If I develop this habit, I will take time to think about what I've just read. Deciding what I think and what I feel helps me remember it better.

Which **STRATEGY** will I use to practice this habit?

Decide whether I like the main character or not.

📝 Use the **After I Read Strategy Sheet** for "Paul Bunyan" on page 26 in the *Strategy Practice Book* to help you react to what you've read.

Apply 3 of the 9 Habits

Now read "Pecos Bill" and apply these three habits and strategies.

Before I Read

Which **HABIT** will I apply?
Decide what I need to know.

Which **STRATEGY** will I use to apply this habit?
Use the genre to decide what might happen in the story.

While I Read

Which **HABIT** will I apply?
Stop and ask, "Does it make sense?"

Which **STRATEGY** will I use to apply this habit?
Decide if what's happening fits with the genre.

After I Read

Which **HABIT** will I apply?
React to what I've read.

Which **STRATEGY** will I use to apply this habit?
Decide whether I like the main character or not.

Use the **Self-Assessment Sheet** for "Pecos Bill" on pages 27–28 in the *Strategy Practice Book* as you read to see how well you can apply the habits and strategies.

Pecos Bill

There aren't many cowboys around these days, not the ridin', ropin', rootin'-tootin' kind of the old days. But those few **lingering** cowboys like to remember the greatest of them all, the man who practically invented cowboys, Pecos Bill.

When Bill was born he already had 13 brothers and sisters. His family lived smack-dab in the center of a great **prairie**. And that's just how they liked it. So you can imagine that when another family moved in 300 miles away, they had no choice but to move. The prairie was getting just too blasted crowded. So they loaded up the wagon and headed out.

lingering
(**ling**•guh•ring)—
being slow to leave;
remaining

prairie (**prair**•ee)—a
large area of grassy
land

As the family crossed the Pecos River, Baby Bill threw out his fishing line to catch some lunch. Faster than a Texas jackrabbit, a big ol' trout jumped up, bit the line, and jerked Bill out of the wagon. The fish might still be tugging Bill upstream if it hadn't been for a pack of coyotes that pulled Bill out of the water.

The coyotes were good to Bill. They taught him everything they knew about being wild. It didn't take long for Bill to get to feeling like a part of the pack.

Then one day, Bill saw a strange creature. It was a man and, judging by the way he stared at Bill, he must have thought Bill was mighty strange, too. He spoke to Bill. "You're naked as a jaybird. Where are your clothes?"

"Coyotes don't wear clothes," answered Bill.

"Coyote! You ain't no coyote," laughed the stranger.

"Then what am I?" asked Bill.

"You're a Texan!"

That sounded pretty good to Bill. So he took the clothes the man offered him and off he went to find adventure.

Not too far down the trail, Bill was attacked by a 50-foot rattlesnake. But Bill was quick. He grabbed the snake and squeezed. All the snake's poison drained from its body. It practically **wilted** in Bill's hand. Without its poison, that snake was gentle as a kitten. "Looky here," Bill said. "I been needin' a rope." Then he coiled the snake up and slung it over his shoulder. It wasn't long before he got to try it out.

Somewhere in the Hill Country, Bill ran into a cougar. It didn't take much more than a few seconds for Bill to lasso the big cat. Then Bill jumped on its back and hollered, "Giddap!" The cat didn't like it much, but what could he do? They took off through the hills with Bill hootin' and hollerin' all the way.

After a spell, Bill happened upon a camp. As soon as he smelled the pork and beans cooking over the fire, he realized he was hungry. He slid off the cougar, strode over to the fire, lifted the pot of beans and swallowed them in one gulp. He picked up a pot of boiling coffee and poured it straight down his throat. Then he noticed that the men in the camp were watching him.

wilted (**wil**·tid)— became weak and floppy

"Who's the boss o' this here outfit?" Bill asked.

One gruff-looking man called Sourdough stepped forward. "I was, till a minute ago. Now I reckon you are."

Bill smiled. "Well, then. What exactly is it you boys do?"

"Well, we call ourselves the Dry Gulch Gang. Mostly we just sit around and eat beans and drink coffee. Sometimes we do a little ridin'."

"That don't seem too interestin'," said Bill. "From now on you boys are cowboys. You see all them **longhorns** out there?" Bill pointed to a herd of cattle wandering across the Texas prairie. "We're gonna round 'em up and take 'em to Kansas."

Sourdough and the others looked a little **skeptical**. "How do you aim for us to do that?"

Bill took the snake from his shoulder, swung it over his head, and then flung it out so that it rested around the horns of a passing longhorn. "Like that," said Bill. "I just invented cattle ropin'!" Then he let out one of his wild coyote howls that scared the just-roped

longhorns
(**long**·hornz)—a type of cattle that lives in the Southwest

skeptical
(**skep**·ti·kuhl)— disbelieving

bull right out of its skin. The bull was so embarrassed that he ran behind a mesquite tree to hide. Bill cut the bull's hide into long, thin strips. Then he handed the strips out to his new cowboys to use as ropes.

Most folks say that what happened next was the very first western rodeo. Bill and his gang of cowboys got to flingin' their ropes and scufflin' and tumblin' with every longhorn in sight. By the end of the day, they were swearin' on their mamma's biscuits that they'd round up every last cow in Texas if that's what Bill wanted.

And so the roundup began. Then Bill invented the cattle drive. He and the boys were taking the herd to Kansas. But Bill needed something to ride besides the cougar. The cowboys were afraid of it, and the cows got spooked every time Bill rode by.

The first time Bill laid eyes on Widow-Maker, he knew that horse was the only one for him. Unfortunately, Widow-Maker didn't share Bill's feelings. "You mangy ol' polecat," said Widow-Maker in horse language. "You ain't ridin' on my back." Then he reared up and ran off in a cloud of West Texas dust.

Naturally, Bill didn't give up. He chased Widow-Maker down. "Whoa there, boy," Bill said, because he knew horse language, too. "I know you're the finest horse anywhere. You know I'm the rootin' tootinest cowboy anywhere. The sooner we team up, the better off we'll both be." So Bill and Widow-Maker became partners.

Everything was ready, and Pecos Bill and his Dry Gulch Gang made the first cattle drive. Along the way, Bill taught the boys all they could learn about ropin' and ridin'. He taught them how to howl like coyotes around the campfire at night. Bill thought life was pretty sweet, until one day, when he started to cross the Rio Grande River. Ridin' down the river on the back of a big ol' Texas catfish was the prettiest girl he'd ever laid eyes on. It was Slewfoot Sue. But that, pardners, starts a whole new story.

Put Your Habits to Work in

Literature | **Social Studies** | **Science** | **Math**

Before I Read Habit:
Decide what I need to know.

Think about the genre as a way of deciding what you need to know about this topic. This will help you focus your reading better, which will improve your understanding and recall of the selection.

Eastward, Ho!

While I Read Habit:
Stop and ask, "Does it make sense?"

As you go along, decide whether what's happening fits with the genre to check on your understanding of the selection.

> In the yard the boys listened to last-minute instructions from Felix, the trail boss. As the sun rose, George Rennick, riding his best horse, appeared leading Hannibal on a rope. Saddle leather creaked, and horses snorted in the crisp air, as the young riders took their places.

After I Read Habit:
React to what I've read.

Take time to think about whether you liked the main character to help you remember the selection better.

> I think the main character . . .

You may wish to use the **Put Your Habits to Work Sheet** on page 29 in your *Strategy Practice Book* to practice these habits in your other reading.

Unit 5
Pioneers in Technology
Theme: Imagination

In this unit, you will develop these 3 habits for all readers.

Before I Read Habit:
Check it out!

While I Read Habit:
Stop and ask, "How does it connect to what I know?"

After I Read Habit:
Use what I've read.

Learn 3 of the 9 Habits

In this unit, you will work on three habits—one for before you read, one for while you are reading, and one for after you finish reading. Start with **Before I Read**. Read the habit and strategy. Then read my notes below.

Before I Read

Which **HABIT** will I learn?
Check it out!
If I develop this habit, I can find out something about what I am going to read so that I know what to expect.

Which **STRATEGY** will I use to learn this habit?
Identify the genre.

My Notes

- Strategy says to identify the genre. Genre is the category of fiction or nonfiction that the selection belongs to.
- The title says "A Real Television Hero," so it might be about a person.
- I looked at the first paragraph of the story and saw that it was about someone named Philo Farnsworth.
- I decided then that it is about a real person's life.
- Then I decided that the genre is biography, because it is a true story about a real person.

A Real Television Hero

Philo Farnsworth with an early model of his invention

Philo [**fie**•loh] Farnsworth changed your life, but you have probably never heard of him. He was born in a log cabin in Utah in 1906. However, Philo did not live there long. He and his family moved to a small town, to a farm, to another small town, to Salt Lake City, to more small towns, and finally to his uncle's ranch in Idaho. The family made several of these moves in wagons pulled by horses. Some people had cars back then, but Philo's family could not afford one.

By the time Philo died in 1971, he not only had a car of his own, he also held 165 **patents** on his inventions. Philo was a pioneer in the development of television.

patent (pat•uhnt)—a paper giving only the holder of the patent the right to make, use, or sell an invention

While I Read

Which **HABIT** will I learn?

Stop and ask, "How does it connect to what I know?"

If I develop this habit, I will think about how what I'm reading fits with what I know. This helps me understand the new material and remember it better.

Which **STRATEGY** will I use to learn this habit?

Design a graphic organizer.

generator
(**jen**•uh•ray•tur)—a machine that changes the energy of movement into useful electricity

Stop and Ask ❓

How does it connect to what I know? Design a graphic organizer.

I started a web with the name "Philo Farnsworth" in the middle. I drew lines to two other circles. One circle says "Childhood." The other says, "On Uncle's Ranch." I added details inside those circles. For example, in "Childhood," I put "Born in 1906."

Drawn by Electricity

Philo's fascination with electricity began the first time he saw electric toy trains and electric motors in a Sears catalog. Yet his family did not have electricity until they moved to his uncle's ranch in 1919. At that time, Philo was 13.

He quickly found the **generator** that produced electricity for the ranch. From then on, Philo spent all his spare time experimenting with the generator. He often caused it to stop working. Some weeks, his mother had to call for repairs two or three times to get the generator fixed.

During these repair visits, Philo paid close attention to how the repairs were made. Soon, he was able to repair it himself. Then he started connecting other machines to the generator. Once he figured everything out, he hooked up his mother's washing machine to the generator. Next, Philo hooked up his mother's sewing machine. Soon the generator did all of the work! Then he added electric lights to his uncle's barn. Young Philo was soon asked to wire other buildings in town for electricity. ❓ *Strategy Alert!*

To learn more about electricity, Philo read all the science magazines he could find. Although most people did not yet have radios, Philo read about an idea for **transmitting** pictures, called television. Now that was exciting—a machine that could receive pictures! He decided to see if he could make a television.

While Philo was experimenting with his ideas, he entered a contest. The Ford Motor Company was offering $25 for an invention to improve the automobile. Well, $25 was a lot of money back then. Philo's family still did not have a car, but he had an idea for a way to start a car without **cranking** it. He invented an **ignition** that would start the car only if a special key was used. The key had to be **magnetized** by electricity. He had used what he knew about electricity to win the prize. And now thieves would not be able to steal cars with a simple turn of the crank.

? *Strategy Alert!*

The Ford Model T

transmitting
(trans•**mit**•ing)—
sending from one place to another by radio waves or wire

cranking (**krang**•king)
—starting a car by turning on the engine with a crank in the front

ignition
(ig•**ni**•shuhn)—the part of a car that makes it start

magnetized
(**mag**•nuh•tiezd)—able to attract metals; many metals are magnetized when electricity passes through them

Stop and Ask ?

How does it connect to what I know? Design a graphic organizer.

• • • • • • • • • • • •

I added a circle to the web called "Early Inventions." In it I wrote, "Ignition with special key."

The Picture Becomes Clearer

In 1920, when Philo was in the ninth grade, he was allowed to take a twelfth-grade science class. His teacher was amazed at Philo's questions. Philo was not just curious. He was looking for ways to send pictures over wires.

One day, Philo was **plowing** a field at his uncle's ranch. He noticed the pattern of straight lines he was making in the soil. What if he divided a picture into small pieces, the way the lines were dividing the field? Then he could change each piece of the picture into a bit of electricity and send it through a wire. When the bits of electricity reached the television set, they could be changed back into pieces of the picture.

Straight lines in the soil (left) gave Philo an idea. He could divide a picture into straight lines. Straight lines (above) make up the picture on our television screens.

Philo was really excited about his idea. With his science teacher's help, he learned about special glass tubes called **cathode-ray tubes**. All the air is removed from these tubes. Because of this and what he knew about electricity, he was sure that his pieces of pictures would be able to move more easily.

At the age of 14, Philo used a cathode-ray tube in his design for an electronic television. It was made of a television camera and a television receiver. In the camera, the picture would be divided up and changed into a pattern of electricity. In the receiver (the cathode-ray tube), the pattern of electricity would be changed back into a picture. **?** *Strategy Alert!*

---

plowing (plow•ing)— breaking up soil in rows for planting crops

cathode-ray tubes (**kath**•ohd-ray toobz)— glass tubes from which all of the air has been removed, which are coated with a glowing substance that produces light at a certain point on a screen when electricity flows through the tubes

---

Stop and Ask **?**

How does it connect to what I know? Design a graphic organizer.

· · · · · · · · · ·

I added a circle that said, "Philo's First TV." Then I wrote inside the circle, "Plowing," "Science teacher," and "Cathode-ray tubes." Those are things that helped Philo with his invention.

A Bumpy Road to Success

When he was 15, Philo started college at Brigham Young University in Utah. However, he did not stay long. He had too many ideas to try out. Soon, he was able to produce his first receiver. It measured only 4 inches across. The picture was in black and white.

In 1927, at the age of 21, Philo applied for a patent for his television invention so no one else could use his idea. In 1934, a British company bought a license from Philo so it could use his design. In 1939, the Radio Corporation of America (RCA) also bought a license from Philo. Then the British company and RCA competed with each other and with Philo to make the first television sets for the public. Unfortunately, Philo did not have enough money or staff to keep up with these huge companies, so the companies were the ones who made the money from Philo's invention.

By the end of World War II in 1945, television was no longer a strange idea. Television shows were being **broadcast** daily. Televisions were beginning to appear in people's homes. Philo spent his time working on ways to improve his original idea. For example, he discovered a way to make a cathode-ray tube that would not heat up. ❓ *Strategy Alert!*

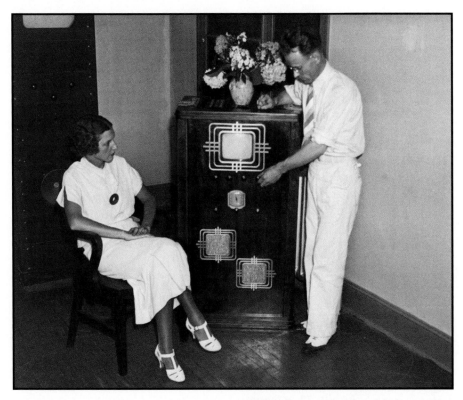

Philo demonstrating his invention

broadcast (**brawd**•kast)—sent out by means of television or radio signals

Stop and Ask ❓

How does it connect to what I know? Design a graphic organizer.

● ● ● ● ● ● ● ● ● ● ● ●

I added a circle to my web that said, "Later Inventions." Inside it I put, "Television set for the public," "TV improvements," and "Cool cathode-ray tube."

microscope
(**mie**•kruh•skohp)—a device that allows you to see a larger image of a very small thing

atomic energy
(uh•**tahm**•ik en•ur•jee)—energy made when the tiniest parts of matter split or join

Stop and Ask ?

How does it connect to what I know? Design a graphic organizer.

○ ○ ○ ○ ○ ○ ○ ○ ○ ○ ○ ○

I put in a circle that said, "Life Accomplishments." Inside it I wrote, "165 patents" and "Saw astronauts walk on moon on his own invention."

Looking Back

Philo did not see electricity in use until he was 13. However, he had already thought of many ways he could put it to work. His ideas led to 165 patents, mostly in radio and television. However, he invented something for medicine, too—an electronic **microscope**. He even did research in **atomic energy**.

In 1969, Philo Farnsworth watched as television showed the first astronauts walking on the moon. "This has made it all worthwhile," he told his wife. Philo had never dreamed of traveling to the moon. However, his ideas helped us see that first step on the moon and many other things. The next time you turn on your television, thank Philo. ? *Strategy Alert!*

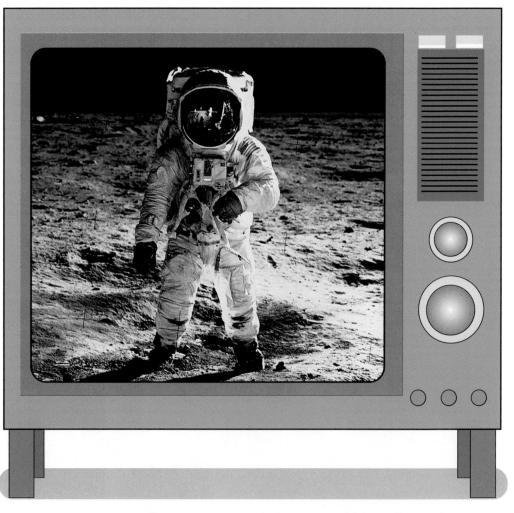

Apollo 11 astronaut Edwin "Buzz" Aldrin walks on the moon.

Now read the habit and strategy for **After I Read**. Then read my notes below.

After I Read

Which **HABIT** will I learn?
Use what I've read.
If I develop this habit, I will think about how I can apply what I just read to my schoolwork and my life. This makes reading really useful.

Which **STRATEGY** will I use to learn this habit?
Tell what I learned about the central character.

My Notes

- Strategy says to tell what I learned about the central character. The central character was Philo Farnsworth.

- He was very interested in how electricity made things work.

- He invented television.

- Philo's inventions changed the world.

Now it's time to practice the three habits and strategies you learned when you read "A Real Television Hero." Reread the habit and strategy below and then do it!

Before I Read

Which **HABIT** will I practice?
Check it out!

> If I develop this habit, I can find out something about what I am going to read so that I know what to expect.

Which **STRATEGY** will I use to practice this habit?

> Identify the genre.

 Use the **Before I Read Strategy Sheet** for "Weaving the World Together" on page 30 in the *Strategy Practice Book* to help you check it out.

WEAVING THE WORLD TOGETHER

How do you use the World Wide Web? Do you look for information for school reports? Do you do searches on topics that interest you? Do you e-mail your friends and family members? Do you sometimes shop **on-line**? Today, millions of people use the Web. It was invented by a man named Tim Berners-Lee. He proposed the idea of the World Wide Web in 1989. In 1991, computer users were first able to use the Web. Now it's an important part of modern life.

The Web or the Internet?

Do you know the difference between the Web and the Internet? They are not the same. The Internet is a network of networks, made from computers and cables. The Web is a way to send information over the Internet. The Web is made of **documents** and **files**. The Internet provides the connections so the documents and files of the Web can be delivered where they are sent.

on-line—connected through a system, especially a computer system

documents (**dahk•yoo•muhnts**)—pieces of writing that convey information, whether electronically or on paper

files—groups of documents stored together, whether electronically or in paper file folders

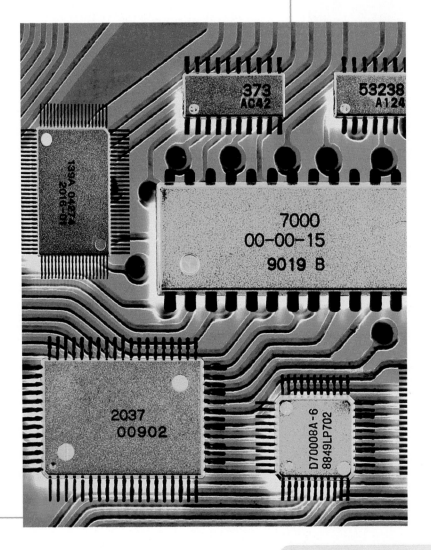

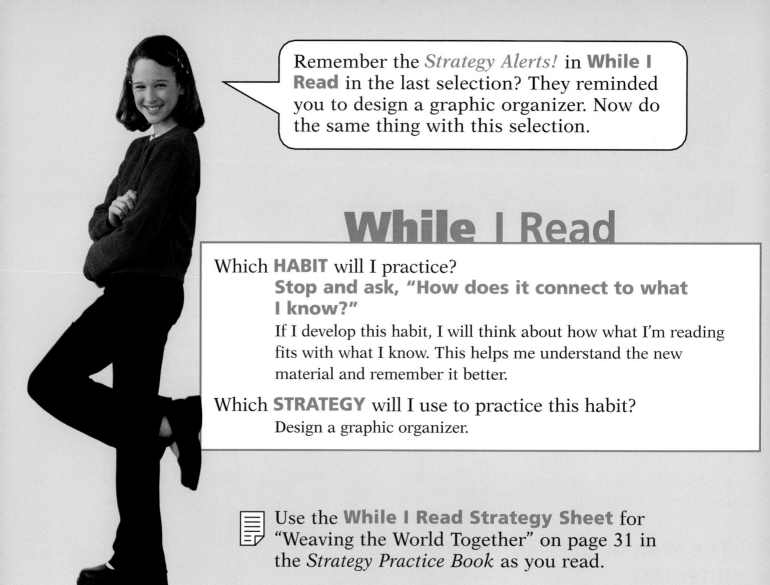

Remember the *Strategy Alerts!* in **While I Read** in the last selection? They reminded you to design a graphic organizer. Now do the same thing with this selection.

While I Read

Which **HABIT** will I practice?
Stop and ask, "How does it connect to what I know?"
If I develop this habit, I will think about how what I'm reading fits with what I know. This helps me understand the new material and remember it better.

Which **STRATEGY** will I use to practice this habit?
Design a graphic organizer.

Use the **While I Read Strategy Sheet** for "Weaving the World Together" on page 31 in the *Strategy Practice Book* as you read.

Stop and Ask

How does it connect to what I know? Design a graphic organizer.

mathematicians
(math•muh•**tish**•uhnz)
—people who are experts in math

Tim Berners-Lee makes it clear that he did not invent the Internet. The Internet was designed in 1973 by a number of people. After 10 years of improvements, it was made available for public use in 1983. Tim stresses that his Web could not exist without the Internet. The Web depends on the connections provided by the Internet. **?** *Strategy Alert!*

How the Web Was Woven

Tim was born in 1955 in London, England. His parents were both **mathematicians**. They met while they were helping to develop the first kind of computer to be sold in stores.

As a child, Tim loved knowing how electricity makes things work. When he entered The Queen's College at Oxford University, he studied **physics**. He believes that his background in physics has helped him think in clear, planned ways. Tim graduated in 1976. For the next several years, he worked for computer companies, designing **software** and computer systems.

By 1990, Tim was working for CERN, a physics laboratory in Switzerland. While there, he invented a new kind of notebook for himself. He used it to keep track of the people and projects he was working with and how they were connected. This pioneer of the computer age then used the idea behind his notebook to create a model of the Web. He designed the Web as a way to combine or link documents by using hypertext. A hypertext document contains links to other documents. If you click on a certain word or phrase in a hypertext document, a related document will appear on your computer screen. Often, the hypertext is printed in blue to make it easy to locate. Hypertext helps people work together by linking their knowledge in a web.  *Strategy Alert!*

physics (fiz·iks)—the study of matter and energy and how they interact

software (sawft·wair)—computer programs; the codes that tell a computer what to do

Stop and Ask ?

How does it connect to what I know? Design a graphic organizer.

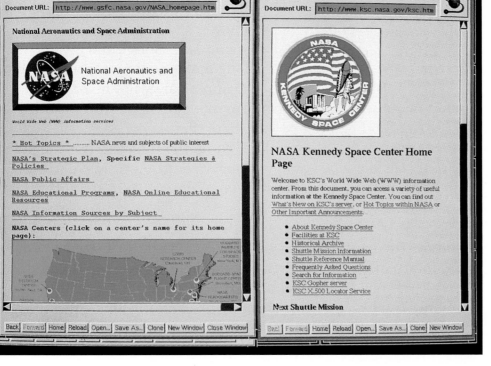

The home pages of NASA and the Kennedy Space Center

consortium
(kuhn•**sor**•shuhm)—a group that is formed to perform a task no one member could do alone

Stop and Ask ?

How does it connect to what I know? Design a graphic organizer.

In August of 1991, Tim put his new Web on the Internet. It immediately attracted users and continues to do so. In 1994, Tim went to work for the Laboratory for Computer Science at the Massachusetts Institute of Technology. He is now in charge of the World Wide Web **Consortium** (W3C). This group is responsible for guiding the development of the Web and helping it reach its potential. It sets standards for the Web, including the kinds of technology that can be used. It also settles disagreements related to the Web and its use. In this way, W3C helps keep the Web from breaking into many smaller webs. If it broke up, communication between webs would be complicated and difficult. It might not even be possible to move information from one web to another. ? *Strategy Alert!*

Tim Berners-Lee

Praise for a Pioneer

As the Web continues to pull us all together, *Time* magazine has chosen Tim as one of the great minds of the twentieth century. *Time* says that the full effect of Tim's pioneering work will not be known for years. The list of Tim's awards is long and growing, as people begin to appreciate what he has done.

You might wonder whether Tim made millions from his idea for linking sites and helping people share their knowledge. The answer is no. As soon as he entered the Web on the Internet, it belonged to everyone. He knew he could no longer control it or make money from it. Although the W3C tries to maintain certain standards, no one owns the World Wide Web.

Because of this lack of control, Web sites are not checked for accuracy. Tim cautions Web users to watch out for biased or one-sided information. Some sites, for example, are personal Web pages. They may look **official,** but they offer only the owners' opinions. Tim urges Web users to think carefully about the information offered by all sites. You can't assume something is correct just because it is on the Web. ? *Strategy Alert!*

official
(uh•**fish**•uhl)—coming from an authority

Stop and Ask ?

How does it connect to what I know? Design a graphic organizer.

Still, he is pleased with the way his idea has taken shape and taken off. He believes that the Web allows people to communicate and work together in ways no one imagined 50 years ago. This communication, Tim believes, may lead to many needed changes. In time, the Web might change how people are elected to government offices or how businesses are run. It has already made changes in the way we do business, the way we exchange ideas, and even the way we shop and entertain ourselves. Tim is satisfied that his contribution, the World Wide Web, will be a major influence on our lives from now on. That's payment enough for him. **?** *Strategy Alert!*

Stop and Ask

How does it connect to what I know? Design a graphic organizer.

Remember that you're not finished until you've used what you've read.

After I Read

Which **HABIT** will I practice?
Use what I've read.

If I develop this habit, I will think about how I can apply what I just read to my schoolwork and my life. This makes reading really useful.

Which **STRATEGY** will I use to practice this habit?

Tell what I learned about the central character.

Use the **After I Read Strategy Sheet** for "Weaving the World Together" on page 32 in the *Strategy Practice Book* to help you use what you've read.

Apply 3 of the 9 Habits

Now read "Pioneering a New Language" and apply these three habits and strategies.

Before I Read

Which **HABIT** will I apply?
Check it out!

Which **STRATEGY** will I use to apply this habit?
Identify the genre.

While I Read

Which **HABIT** will I apply?
Stop and ask, "How does it connect to what I know?"

Which **STRATEGY** will I use to apply this habit?
Design a graphic organizer.

After I Read

Which **HABIT** will I apply?
Use what I've read.

Which **STRATEGY** will I use to apply this habit?
Tell what I learned about the central character.

Use the **Self-Assessment Sheet** for "Pioneering a New Language" on pages 33–34 in the *Strategy Practice Book* as you read to see how well you can apply the habits and strategies.

Pioneering a New Language

Augusta Ada Byron King, Countess of Lovelace, known as Ada, had a strange start for a pioneer. She was born into a wealthy London family in 1815. Ada was the child of the famous English poet Lord Byron. Her mother also came from a wealthy family. At that time, the only thing that British society seemed to expect from wealthy girls and women was a pleasant smile and good manners. As a teenager, Ada spent much of her time attending plays, going to parties, and dancing at balls.

Yet Ada became one of the very few women mathematicians of her time. She was the world's first computer programmer, male or female. In 1979, the United States Department of Defense named its main computer language Ada after her.

An Unusual Beginning

Ada never knew her father, Lord Byron. He was a difficult man, full of anger and other stormy emotions. He and his wife couldn't get along. When Ada was only 7 weeks old, she and her mother went to live with her mother's parents. Several weeks later, Lord Byron left England and never again saw his wife or daughter. Ada's mother raised her with the help of Ada's grandparents. Lord Byron died in Greece when Ada was 8 years old. During the early 1800s, the daughters of wealthy British families were required to learn the **"social graces."** They needed to prepare for all the parties they would attend. These young women studied music, painting, and languages. Ada, however, preferred museums and **lectures** to parties. When she was only 5 years old, she was able to add 6 rows of numbers. Before she turned 13, she was studying **geometry**. Her mother was also interested in math and encouraged Ada's interest. Ada was taught at home by private tutors. Later, she studied on her own.

Math Leads to Computers

At one of many parties, Ada happened to meet Charles Babbage, a scientist, mathematician, and inventor. One of his inventions is the speedometer, a device that tells drivers how fast they are going. He also invented the skeleton key, a key that can open any door.

Babbage also invented the ophthalmoscope, an instrument that allows doctors to look at the back of the eye. In addition, he created a machine that could solve math problems and print the answers. He called this invention the "Analytical Engine." Ada visited his home and saw a model of the machine. She immediately understood how it worked. Babbage and Ada decided to work together.

A car speedometer and odometer

social graces (**soh**•shuhl **grays**•uhz) —the skills involved in getting along at social events

lectures (**lek**•churz)—informative talks on serious topics

geometry (jee•**ahm**•uh•tree) —the part of mathematics that deals with the measurement and relationships of points, lines, and angles in surfaces and solids

A doctor tests a young patient's eyes

At first, the British government gave Babbage money to build his engine. Then the government changed its mind and decided not to support the project. He didn't mind. He already had an idea for a new invention, which would become the first computer. It would be able to read and store information, solve math problems, carry out the user's instructions, and print the answers.

Charles Babbage's invention was never built, partly because it was too far ahead of its time. The technology in the mid-1800s could not turn his ideas into a working machine. Also, the British government was not interested in paying for any more of his projects. Nevertheless, Ada wrote sets of instructions for solving math problems using this machine. Today we would call this computer programming. Ada wrote programs for Babbage's machine even though it was never built.

In her early 20s, Ada married William King, also known as Lord Lovelace. He was proud of her achievements and encouraged her work. In those days, most women did not work in math or science. Ada decided to sign her work "A.A.L." instead of using her name. Few people knew that those were the initials of Augusta Ada Byron King, Countess of Lovelace.

Charles Babbage

organization
(org•uh•nuh•**zay**•shuhn)
—the quality of being
organized

Over the years, Ada continued to work with Charles Babbage off and on. However, she was greatly bothered by his careless work habits and lack of **organization**. At one point, she asked him to sign an agreement to change his ways. He refused. But they did work together on another project. They tried to develop a mathematical system to figure out the winners in horse races. Their system did not work! Unfortunately, Ada lost money when she placed bets using the system. She even had to sell some of her jewels to pay what she owed.

In her 30s, Ada became sick with cancer. She died of the disease in 1852. She was only 36 years old. That is the same age at which her father died.

Ada's Legacy

Imagine what Ada might say if she were alive today and could walk through a manufacturing plant, a laboratory, a mall, an office, or even a home. She would probably be amazed at how computers have influenced our lives. She might also be pleased at the way the United States Department of Defense honored her contributions to computer technology. Ada did not write the programming language that the Department of Defense named after her, but her work helped make modern computer programming possible.

Ada did have some idea of how her work might be used someday. However, she warned against depending too much on computers. She wrote that they can do only what we program them to do. They do not think for themselves, so we must be careful!

One hundred and fifty years after Ada's death, we have a shorter way to say this: "Garbage in, garbage out." Computer programmers and users still have to do a lot of thinking. If they put in errors, they get errors back.

Put Your Habits to Work in

Literature | **Social Studies** | **Science** | **Math**

Before I Read Habit:
Check it out!

Decide what genre the selection belongs to. This will give you an idea of how you should read it.

While I Read Habit:
Stop and ask, "How does it connect to what I know?"

As you go along, make a graphic organizer that shows the main ideas in the selection.

After I Read Habit:
Use what I've read.

Tell what you learned about the central character as a way of showing that you understood the selection.

The main character was . . .

You may wish to use the **Put Your Habits to Work Sheet** on page 35 in your *Strategy Practice Book* to practice these habits in your other reading.

Unit 6
Your Heritage, Our Heritage
Theme: Myself

In this unit, you will develop these 3 habits for all readers.

Before I Read Habit:
Check it out!

While I Read Habit:
Stop and ask, "If it doesn't make sense, what can I do?"

After I Read Habit:
Check to see what I remember.

Learn 3 of the 9 Habits

In this unit, you will work on three habits—one for before you read, one for while you are reading, and one for after you finish reading. Start with **Before I Read**. Read the habit and strategy. Then read my notes below.

Before I Read

Which **HABIT** will I learn?
Check it out!
If I develop this habit, I can find out something about what I am going to read so that I know what to expect.

Which **STRATEGY** will I use to learn this habit?
Skim the summary and predict what the selection will be about.

My Notes

- Strategy says to skim the summary and predict what I'll be reading about.
- The summary talks about how you can learn about different foods that people cook and eat.
- The summary also talks about cooking and eating around the world.
- I think this will be about foods that people eat in different parts of the world.

The Great Salad Bowl

"Grandma Rose, what smells so good?" Jonathan let the screen door slam shut behind him. Grandma Rose usually watched him after school. "What are you cooking?"

Grandma Rose scraped some small pieces of onion from her cutting board into a frying pan. They sizzled in hot peanut oil. "I'm making something special tonight, sweetie-pie! All the cousins are coming over. We're going to have all the foods my momma and daddy used to make back in **Jamaica**." She sniffed and wiped her eyes on the corner of a dish towel—the onions had gotten to her. She pushed a strand of gray hair off her face with the back of her hand. "And you are coming, too!"

Jonathan looked at the foods Grandma Rose had put out to cook with. "Good!" he said. On the counter were a green bell pepper, a red bell pepper, a bottle of hot sauce, and, of course, the onion. These were foods Jonathan approved of. Jonathan's mouth began to water. But there were two bowls that contained things Jonathan hadn't seen before.

Jamaica (juh•**may**•kuh) —an island in the Caribbean

Now read the habit and strategy for **While I Read**. When you see ❓, read my notes in the margin.

While I Read

Which **HABIT** will I learn?

Stop and ask, "If it doesn't make sense, what can I do?"

If I develop this habit, I will stop and figure out what to do so what I'm reading makes sense. Then I can keep reading and not be lost.

Which **STRATEGY** will I use to learn this habit?

Slow down when the reading gets difficult.

Learning About a New Food

"What's that lumpy yellow stuff?" Jonathan asked, wrinkling his nose. "And what's that white flaky stuff?"

"Well, Jonathan, those are the things this recipe is named for. It's called **ackee** and salt fish." She picked up the bowl of yellow stuff. "This is the ackee. It's a fruit from Africa that grows now in Jamaica. It's good." She paused to stir the onions. "This white stuff is codfish that's been salted and dried. I soaked it all night and all day to get the salt out!"

Grandma Rose cut into the peppers and took out the seeds. Then she started **dicing**. "Once I get everything all cut up, I'll toss it all together in this frying pan until it's hot. It'll look like scrambled eggs—and taste like them, too!"

ackee (ak•ee)—a fleshy fruit that is yellow on the inside and grows in parts of Africa and in the Caribbean

dicing (die•sing)—cutting into very small pieces

She wiped her hands and leaned against the countertop. "When I was a little girl, we grew peppers and onions in our own yard. This was in **Kingston**. We could pick ackee from the trees out back of the house. You had to know just when the fruit was ripe or it would poison you! We liked knowing the ackee tree came from Africa just like we did."  *Strategy Alert!*

Learning About Yourself

The people living in the United States are like the parts of a great big tossed salad. In a salad, there are many separate **ingredients**. Each one keeps its own flavor and color. But, when put together, they make a whole new flavor that is very appealing. Every time new people arrive, they add new flavors and new ingredients.

Where did the first people living in the U.S. come from? People probably first came from Asia and spread throughout the Americas. This was thousands of years ago. Many of these people were probably the early ancestors of our present-day Native Americans. In the 1500s, European people started arriving. That started wave after wave of new arrivals. Today, many people are arriving from Mexico, Central America, and South America. Many people from Asia and India are also arriving.

Kingston (king•stuhn)— the capital of Jamaica

Stop and Ask ?

If it doesn't make sense, what can I do? Slow down when the reading gets difficult.

It was hard to understand what Grandma Rose was saying. When I slow down, I can understand that Grandma Rose is talking about her childhood in Jamaica and that her family came from Africa.

ingredients (in•**greed**•ee•uhnts)— the different foods and seasonings that make up a recipe

Stop and Ask ?

If it doesn't make sense, what can I do? Slow down when the reading gets difficult.

· · · · · · · · · · · ·

The story changed and I needed to slow down to make sure it made sense. Now it's talking about the story of many people, not just Grandma Rose's story. It's talking about people who moved to the United States from all over the world.

The United States is an exciting mix of people from all over the world. It is a salad bowl of people from many lands. Where did your family come from? What flavor does your family add to the salad bowl? ? *Strategy Alert!*

You can find out a lot about your roots by cooking and eating and talking about food. You can find out why your family eats certain foods. You can find out if the older people in your community grew up in the United States or came here from somewhere else. Ask them if they will share a meal or a recipe with you. Finding out the favorite recipes of your family and your community is a good way to get to know your own history—the part you play in the salad bowl. Maybe you can fix a meal from an old recipe and invite some people from your community over to talk and eat with you. Or invite some of your friends over and share the foods of your culture with others. ? *Strategy Alert!*

Stop and Ask ?

If it doesn't make sense, what can I do? Slow down when the reading gets difficult.

· · · · · · · · · · · ·

I slowed down for this paragraph, too. It talks about getting to know my own history by asking about the foods my family ate. I can talk to my own grandma, just like Jonathan was talking to his.

Learning About Others

The next day, Jonathan was back. "Hi, Grandma Rose," he yelled. Again, he let the screen door slam shut behind him. Jonathan went right to the refrigerator. He opened the door and stuck his head inside.

"Let me guess," Grandma Rose said, coming into the room. "You're hungry!"

"I sure am," Jonathan said from inside the refrigerator. "And you must have some great leftovers from our **feast** last night!"

They filled two bowls with the bright yellow salt fish and ackee and heated them in the microwave. "Grandma Rose?" Jonathan asked.

"Yes, Jonathan?" she replied.

"My friend Jake at school said that when his family gets together, they eat **shish kebabs** dipped in yogurt! And they eat other interesting stuff.

He said I can come over and eat with them the next time they have a feast. Is that OK?"

"Of course it is, Jonathan," Grandma Rose said. "It's fun to learn about your own family's foods, but it's also fun to learn about other people's foods. Let's invite Jake over the next time the cousins get together." She took another bite of ackee. "OK?"

"OK!"

Strategy Alert!

feast (feest)—a meal with lots of wonderful food

shish kebabs (shish kuh•bahbz)—a meat dish made by putting chunks of meat and vegetables on a long pointed stick and cooking them over a flame

Stop and Ask ❓

If it doesn't make sense, what can I do? Slow down when the reading gets difficult.

• • • • • • • • • •

The story changed again, and I could speed up a little. I slowed down again when Jonathan was talking about shish kebabs. I didn't know what they were.

Summary

The United States is made up of people from many parts of the world. How can cooking and eating together help you learn more about the history of your own family? Ask where the food came from originally. Find out from older family members and people in your community what they ate and how they cooked when they were younger. You may find the things you eat every day go back to your family's roots around the world. ❓ *Strategy Alert!*

Stop and Ask ❓

If it doesn't make sense, what can I do? Slow down when the reading gets difficult.

The story got harder again, so I slowed down. This paragraph tells what the whole story was about. Now I think I understand what a summary is.

Now read the habit and strategy for **After I Read**. Then read my notes below.

After I Read

Which HABIT will I learn?
Check to see what I remember.
If I develop this habit, I will check to see what I remember as soon as I finish reading. It helps me see if I really understood what I read and helps me remember it better, too.

Which STRATEGY will I use to learn this habit?
Answer the questions in the text.

My Notes

- Strategy says to answer the questions.

- I skimmed through the story to look for questions to see if I could answer them.

- I found a question on page 129, and this is how I answered it: "The first people in America probably came from Asia."

- I found a question on page 130, and this is how I answered it: "Some of my family came from Puerto Rico and some came from Ireland."

- I continued to find questions and tried to answer them, but when I got to the question on page 132, I had to read that part of the selection again to be sure I could answer the question. Here's how I answered it: "The food people eat is part of their family background. By cooking and eating with family we can find out more about where our food and recipes came from."

Now it's time to practice the three habits and strategies you learned when you read "The Great Salad Bowl." Reread the habit and strategy below and then do it!

Before I Read

Which **HABIT** will I practice?
Check it out!
If I develop this habit, I can find out something about what I am going to read so that I know what to expect.

Which **STRATEGY** will I use to practice this habit?
Skim the summary and predict what the selection will be about.

Use the **Before I Read Strategy Sheet** for "Many Lands, Many Breads" on page 36 in the *Strategy Practice Book* to help you check it out.

Many Lands, Many Breads

Has anyone in your house ever made bread? Did the smell of its baking make your mouth water? Perhaps you make bread or **tortillas** at your house every day. Maybe there are breads that you only eat at special times of the year. For example, Jewish people eat **matzo** crackers at Passover. Bread has many names. It may be called **injera, lefse, pagach,** or **pita**. It depends on the culture doing the cooking.

There are hundreds of different cultures in the world. There are similarities among them and there are differences. For example, some cultures respect Saturday as a day of rest and religious practice. Other cultures respect Friday or Sunday. Some cultures eat meat. Others are vegetarian. But almost every culture in the world eats some kind of bread.

Different cultures may make their bread with different grains. They may cook their bread in different kinds of ovens. They may make breads of different shapes. But they all make bread. Sometimes the bread is eaten alone. Often, it is used to hold other foods. Have you ever eaten a peanut butter and jelly sandwich? Then you're familiar with this use of bread. What other foods do you hold with bread?

tortillas (tor•tee•yuhz) —round thin bread made in the Americas

matzo (maht•suh)—a bread eaten during the Jewish holiday of Passover; does not contain yeast

injera (in•jair•uh)—a round flat bread eaten in Ethiopia

lefse (lef•suh)—a flat potato bread eaten in Norway

pagach (puh•gahk)— a Ukrainian filled bread

pita (pee•tuh)—a thin flat bread eaten in the Mediterranean countries

Remember the *Strategy Alerts!* in **While I Read** in the last selection? They reminded you to slow down when the reading got difficult. Now do the same thing with this selection.

While I Read

Which **HABIT** will I practice?
Stop and ask, "If it doesn't make sense, what can I do?"
If I develop this habit, I will stop and figure out what to do so what I'm reading makes sense. Then I can keep reading and not be lost.

Which **STRATEGY** will I use to practice this habit?
Slow down when the reading gets difficult.

 Use the **While I Read Strategy Sheet** for "Many Lands, Many Breads" on page 37 in the *Strategy Practice Book* as you read.

The breads described here are just a few of the wonderful breads available in every community. How many of them have you eaten? The next time you go grocery shopping, see how many different kinds of bread you can find.

Ethiopia: Injera

What country has bread that is similar to pancakes? The answer is Ethiopia [ee•thee•**oh**•pee•yuh]—a country on the east coast of Africa. In Ethiopia, the people make a type of bread called injera. Injera is made out of a flour called *teff* [tef]. The word *teff* means "lost." It may be called this because the teff is so light that it is easy to blow it away. Teff is made from millet, a grain that has been grown in East Africa and the Middle East for thousands of years. To make injera, you combine teff with water and soda to make a thin batter.

Making injera is similar to cooking pancakes. First, a small amount of the batter is placed in a hot skillet. Then, the skillet is swirled around to spread the batter into a thin sheet. When the top of the batter starts to be filled with bubbles, the round bread is quickly removed from the skillet and set aside. The process is repeated until you have all the bread you need for a meal. Injera is thin and **spongy**. When you eat Ethiopian food, you hold a piece of injera in your hand and pick up your other food with it.

Other foods from Ethiopia include spiced cheese, **lentils,** and doro wat [**dor**·oh waht] chicken, a dish made from chicken, onions, many different spices, and hard-boiled eggs. Tear off a piece of injera and dig right in.  *Strategy Alert!*

spongy (**spun**·jee)—soft and full of holes, like a sponge

lentils (**lent**·ulz)—flat beans common in the Middle East and Africa

Stop and Ask ?

If it doesn't make sense, what can I do? Slow down when the reading gets difficult.

Germany: Pumpernickel

Germany is a country in northern Europe. The German people make many kinds of bread, including pumpernickel. Pumpernickel is made with rye flour. Rye is a type of grain that is common in Europe. It has a much sharper flavor than wheat. What other ingredients are in pumpernickel? A good recipe includes rye flour, whole wheat flour, white flour, yeast, molasses, and cocoa powder. It seems funny to put cocoa powder in bread, but the cocoa helps give pumpernickel its rich taste as well as its color.

First, you mix the ingredients together in a big bowl. After the dough is mixed, you knead [need] it. To knead the dough, you roll it and punch it with your hands, folding it over itself many times. Then you set the dough aside in a warm place for an hour. During the hour, the yeast causes the dough to expand, or rise. Then you knead the dough again and place it on a baking sheet that has been covered with cornmeal. The cornmeal keeps the bread from sticking to the pan.

After letting the dough rise again, you put the loaf into the oven. It smells wonderful while it's baking. You end up with a very dark, filling bread that is wonderful to eat with soup or to hold a sandwich together. Warm pumpernickel with butter is delicious all by itself.  *Strategy Alert!*

Stop and Ask ?

If it doesn't make sense, what can I do? Slow down when the reading gets difficult.

India: Chapati Bread

What kind of bread puffs up like a balloon? That's what happens to **chapati** from India. India is a large country in Asia. Many kinds of bread are made there, but chapati is one of the most interesting. The ingredients are simple. You need whole wheat flour, white flour, and warm water. The two flours and the water are blended together until a stiff dough is formed. Small pieces of the dough are pinched off and rolled into thin, round pieces about 8 inches across. These are placed on a hot **griddle** for only a few seconds.

Now comes the exciting part. After it leaves the griddle, each chapati is placed directly over an open gas flame. In just a few seconds, each piece of bread puffs up into a big ball!

After cooking, each chapati is brushed with *ghee* [gee]. Ghee is a kind of butter used in many Indian dishes. This wonderful bread is used to pick up other foods in an Indian meal. Those foods might include **chutney** or *dal* [dahl], a dish of peas or lentils cooked with spices. Or you might tear off a piece of chapati to scoop up some chicken *vindaloo* [**vin**•duh•loo], a stew made with chicken, vegetables, and vindaloo, which is a mixture of fourteen different spices. Enjoy! ❓ *Strategy Alert!*

chapati (shuh•**paht**•ee)— a type of bread from India

griddle (**grid**•uhl)—a broad, flat cooking surface

chutney (**chut**•nee)—a thick sauce made in India from fruits and spices or vegetables and spices

Stop and Ask ❓

If it doesn't make sense, what can I do? Slow down when the reading gets difficult.

United States: Cornbread

As people from around the world came to the United States, they brought their breads with them. But are there any breads that were already here in the Americas? One bread that actually comes from the Americas is cornbread. Native Americans taught people from Europe all about how to grow and use corn. Fresh corn is cooked and eaten as a vegetable. Dried corn can be ground into **coarse** flour called cornmeal. Cornbread is made from cornmeal.

coarse (cors)—rough in texture; gritty

You can make rough corn cakes with just cornmeal and water. Cornbread, however, is a little more complicated. A recipe for cornbread might include cornmeal, buttermilk, eggs, bacon fat, and small amounts of sugar, salt, and baking soda. These are mixed together to make a thick, gritty batter. The batter is poured into a hot greased skillet to cook on top of the stove, or it may be baked in an oven.

Wedges or squares of cornbread are often eaten with beans. In the early days of our country, dry cornmeal and dried beans were very important. This is because they were easy for travelers to carry, so they came to be eaten together. All people had to do was add water and they had a satisfying meal. Sometimes cornbread was crumbled right into the beans. Sometimes the beans were poured over pieces of the bread. However, today many people prefer cornbread by itself right out of the oven, with butter melting into it and maybe a dab of jelly on top. ? *Strategy Alert!*

Stop and Ask ?

If it doesn't make sense, what can I do? Slow down when the reading gets difficult.

Summary

Every culture eats some form of bread. One culture may make a loaf that has to be sliced. Another may make flat, round bread such as tortillas. Different grains are used to make different kinds of bread. In Ethiopia, teff is used in making injera. In Germany, rye flour is used to make pumpernickel. People in India use wheat and white flour to make chapati. And in the United States, cornmeal is used to make cornbread.

Remember that you're not finished until you've checked to see what you remember.

After I Read

Which **HABIT** will I practice?
Check to see what I remember.
If I develop this habit, I will check to see what I remember as soon as I finish reading. It helps me see if I really understood what I read and helps me remember it better, too.

Which **STRATEGY** will I use to practice this habit?
Answer the questions in the text.

 Use the **After I Read Strategy Sheet** for "Many Lands, Many Breads" on page 38 in the *Strategy Practice Book* to help you check to see what you remember.

Now read "Foods From the Americas: A Shared Heritage" and apply these three habits and strategies.

Before I Read

Which **HABIT** will I apply?
Check it out!

Which **STRATEGY** will I use to apply this habit?
Skim the summary and predict what the selection will be about.

While I Read

Which **HABIT** will I apply?
Stop and ask, "If it doesn't make sense, what can I do?"

Which **STRATEGY** will I use to apply this habit?
Slow down when the reading gets difficult.

After I Read

Which **HABIT** will I apply?
Check to see what I remember.

Which **STRATEGY** will I use to apply this habit?
Answer the questions in the text.

Use the **Self-Assessment Sheet** for "Foods From the Americas: A Shared Heritage" on pages 39–40 in the *Strategy Practice Book* as you read to see how well you can apply the habits and strategies.

Foods From the Americas: A Shared Heritage

The **archaeologist** stepped back from the area of ground she was uncovering. She put the inch-wide paintbrush she had been using into a pocket of her tool belt and pulled out a tiny artist's brush. Now was the time to work very carefully. She knelt. As she delicately removed a tiny bit of soil at a time, the **relic** could be seen. It was a small string bag. Her team had found several bags just like it. The archaeologist was working at a very old Inca burial place in Peru. The string bag was 1,000 years old. What was inside the burial bag? From other burial places her team had found, the archaeologist guessed that the small bag would contain food. The Inca buried their dead with food to take into the next life.

archaeologist (ahr·kee·**ahl**·uh·jist)—a scientist who studies the places where people lived long ago

relic (**rel**·ik)—a left-over from the distant past

Later that evening, the archaeologist was proven right. The bag contained the foods that were most important to the Inca. It contained peanuts, maize (corn), beans, and peppers. You've probably eaten these foods. Native American people developed these wonderful food crops long before Europeans came to the Americas.

In the years following the arrival of the Europeans, these foods were carried around the globe. Sailors from Spain, Portugal, England, and the Netherlands left American foods in their homelands, but also took them to Africa, India, and Asia. These foods forever changed the way the cultures of the world cooked and ate. Where can the foods of the Americas be found today? They are part of almost every cooking **tradition** in the world. Check what you eat today! You may find that you're eating one of these foods.

tradition
(truh•**dish**•uhn)—the way things are done and have been done in the past

A potato farmer inspects his crop.

Potatoes

The potato was developed as a food crop high in the Andes Mountains where it is cool and damp. It was **domesticated** around 5,000 years ago. The early **Peruvians** had potatoes of many sizes and colors. Their potatoes were white inside but had brown, purple, orange, or pink skins.

The Inca people living in Peru depended on potatoes to survive. Few other crops would grow on the steep mountainsides. The Inca word for potatoes was *papas* [**pah**•puhz].

domesticated
(duh•**mes**•ti•kay•tid)— made useful to humans

Peruvians
(puh•**roo**•vee•uhnz)— the people who live in Peru

In the 1500s, Europeans came to know this potato. They confused it with sweet potatoes, called *batatas* [buh•**tah**•tuhz], which were eaten in the Caribbean. The sweet potato caught on quickly in Europe. Why did the white potato take longer? Europeans thought it might cause diseases. But by the 1800s, the potato was being eaten around the world.

How has the potato influenced history? People living in the country of Ireland came to depend on the potato. When their crops began to die in the middle 1800s, the people had nothing to eat. Many people died. Many left Ireland to come to the United States to live. The Irish were one of the first groups of people to come to the United States in large numbers, as the United States began to be seen as a place of opportunity and freedom. And what did the Irish bring with them? They brought potato recipes, of course.

Tomatoes

The next time you pour a dab of ketchup on a burger, think of ancient Mexico. That's where the tomato was developed several thousand years ago. Spanish **invaders** were the first people from outside the Americas to see the tomato. When they invaded Mexico in 1519, the **Aztec** people were eating several kinds of tomatoes. Where does the word "tomato" come from? It comes from the Aztec word *tomatl* [toh•**mah**•tl]. These early tomatoes were not like the big, shiny red tomatoes we eat today. They were smaller and not as round.

When the Spanish took tomato plants back to Europe, they were grown as **decorative** plants! The Europeans had never seen anything like them, so no one knew how to cook them. Europeans were also afraid that tomatoes might be poisonous. Spain and Italy accepted the tomato more quickly than other European countries.

Today, much of southern Italian cooking depends on the tomato. India and countries in Africa also adopted the tomato. It is the most common fruit grown in China. And, of course, the popularity of tomatoes and foods made with tomatoes continues to grow in the United States. What else do you eat that contains tomatoes or tomato sauce?

invaders (in•**vayd**•urz)—people who move into a country with the purpose of controlling it or taking its goods

Aztec (**az**•tek)—people living in Mexico 500 years ago

decorative (**dek**•uh•ruht•iv)—grown or owned only for beauty, not for food

cayenne (kie·**yen**)—a type of hot pepper

Peppers

Peppers—sweet, hot, green, chili, and **cayenne**—were grown throughout the Americas well before the arrival of Europeans in the 1500s. The Europeans called these foods "peppers" because they were spicy. Pepper was one of the main spices used in Europe at that time. Caribbean people called the fruits of these plants *aji* [**ah**·hee]. The Aztecs in Mexico called them *chilis* [**chee**·leez], a word still associated with chili peppers.

Where did hot peppers first become popular? Europeans found American peppers to be too hot, but people in Asia and Africa loved them. American peppers are important parts of Indian, Chinese, Thai, and many African cooking traditions. In those countries, many people believe that peppers have always grown there. They are not aware that the foods come from the Americas.

When they began to arrive in Europe from Africa and Asia, American peppers began to be accepted. That added to the confusion about where these vegetables actually came from. In the late 1900s, immigrants to the United States from places like Mexico, Thailand, India, and Vietnam brought America's peppers back home. They are very popular today, and some people think "the hotter, the better." Spicy salsa, which is made with peppers, has replaced ketchup as the most popular sauce in the United States.

Maize (Corn)

What was the most important food taken from the Americas? Maize, commonly called corn, was spread around the world. Maize comes from the **Arawak** word *mahiz* [mah·**heez**]. American peoples grew different types of corn and used it in many ways. They boiled it, roasted it, made tortillas from it, and even had a kind of beer made from it. Corn was developed from a wild grass in Mexico 8,000 years ago.

Arawak (**air**·uh·wahk)— people living in the Caribbean in the 1500s

By 1,000 years ago, it was being grown throughout North, South, and Central America. In 1621, the **Wampanoag** Indians taught the English **Pilgrims** how to grow and cook corn, which kept the Pilgrims from starving to death.

Maize grows more quickly than wheat. It also has more **nutrients** in it than wheat. In southern Europe, where many people owned tiny plots of land, corn became very popular. In countries of Africa, corn was adopted quickly. People in **Ghana** and **Congo** eat corn mush. Recipes for corn returned to the Americas when enslaved Africans were brought to the American South. As with peppers, people in African countries and in India and China think of maize as a native food that they have eaten since the earliest times.

Have you had any foods made with maize today? Check the labels before you decide. Corn syrup is used in many foods that don't seem to contain corn.

Summary

Foods from the Americas have spread around the world. When Europeans first arrived in the Americas, the people who lived here were eating potatoes, tomatoes, peppers, and corn, as well as beans, peanuts, and chocolate. These were foods the Europeans had never seen before. The Europeans took the foods back to Europe. They also carried these foods around the world, where they became part of the diet of many different countries and cultures. Many of these foods returned to the Americas when people from other countries immigrated to the United States. Spaghetti? Curry? Putu? The ancient Americans didn't eat these dishes, but they would recognize many of the ingredients. They are part of a food heritage shared by the world.

Wampanoag (wahm•puh•**noh**•ag)— people living in part of New England in the 1600s

Pilgrims (**pil**•gruhmz) —a group of people from England who settled in Massachusetts in the 1620s

nutrients (**noo**•tree•uhnts)—the parts of food that are good for us

Ghana (**gahn**•uh)—a country in West Africa

Congo (**kahn**•goh)—a country in Central Africa

Put Your Habits to Work in

Literature | Social Studies | Science | Math

Before I Read Habit:
Check it out!

Skim the summary and predict what the selection will be about.

While I Read Habit:
Stop and ask, "If it doesn't make sense, what can I do?"

When the reading gets difficult, slow down to think about whether it makes sense.

After I Read Habit:
Check to see what I remember.

Answer the questions in the text.

The answer to that question is . . .

You may wish to use the **Put Your Habits to Work Sheet** on page 41 in your *Strategy Practice Book* to practice these habits in your other reading.

Unit 7
Big Foot and Other Sightings
Theme: Nature

In this unit, you will develop these 3 habits for all readers.

Before I Read Habit:
Think about what I know about the subject.

While I Read Habit:
Stop and ask, "If it doesn't make sense, what can I do?"

After I Read Habit:
React to what I've read.

In this unit, you will work on three habits—one for before you read, one for while you are reading, and one for after you finish reading. Start with **Before I Read**. Read the habit and strategy. Then read my notes below.

Before I Read

Which **HABIT** will I learn?

Think about what I know about the subject.

If I develop this habit, I will bring to mind what I already know about the subject. This gets me ready to connect what I read to what I know so I will understand it better.

Which **STRATEGY** will I use to learn this habit?

Look at the photos and illustrations and decide what I know about what they show.

My Notes

- Strategy says to look at the photos and illustrations and decide what I know about what they show.

- The pictures show a big, hairy, man-like animal.

- I've seen pictures of Big Foot before. It looked a whole lot like these pictures.

- I think this is going to be about Big Foot.

In Search of Big Foot

Big Foot is probably the most famous of all the monsters that exist, or might exist. Actually, there might be several versions of Big Foot. This creature is called Sasquatch (hairy giant) in Canada, the Abominable Snowman and Yeti in the Himalayas and China, and Almas in Mongolia.

Now read the habit and strategy for **While I Read**. When you see ❷, read my notes in the margin.

While I Read

Which **HABIT** will I learn?
Stop and ask, "If it doesn't make sense, what can I do?"
If I develop this habit, I will stop and figure out what to do so what I'm reading makes sense. Then I can keep reading and not be lost.

Which **STRATEGY** will I use to learn this habit?
Use the photos and illustrations to help me understand what I'm reading.

Big Foot is said to be 7 or 8 feet tall and covered with dark brown or reddish-black hair. This monster smells terrible and walks on two feet, like a human. Although people have claimed to see Big Foot for decades, he, or she, was supposedly caught on film in 1967. On October 20 of that year, two friends, Roger Patterson and Bob Gimlin, were riding their horses in northern California. They were following a stream called Bluff Creek. Suddenly, a hairy monster stood up on the other side of the creek. The horses reared in fear, and Patterson was thrown off.

Patterson was able to pull a small movie camera out of his saddlebag and point it at the beast. However, after only a minute of filming, he ran out of film. After the monster disappeared into the woods, the men noticed huge footprints in the sand. They made plaster casts of them. The prints were 14.5 inches long and 5 inches wide. The footprints showed that the monster took steps that were 40 inches apart.

Over the years, experts have tried to prove that Patterson's film was a **hoax**. Even the staff at Walt Disney Studios studied the film because of their expertise in movie trickery. They said they could not have made a film as convincing as that one. 🅰 *Strategy Alert!*

Getting to Know You

Big Foot has been glimpsed many times in the thick forests of northwestern United States and Canada. A Canadian logger named Albert Ostman said that he was kidnapped by Big Foot in 1924! He did not tell anyone for 33 years. He was sure no one would believe him. Ostman said he had been camping near Vancouver Island. He went to sleep by his campfire and woke up being carried inside his sleeping bag! Finally, he was dumped out of the bag in front of a Big Foot family. It included a father, a mother, a boy, and a girl. The family kept him for 6 days, until he managed to escape.

hoax (hohks)—a fake

Stop and Ask ❓

If it doesn't make sense, what can I do? Use the photos and illustrations to help me understand what I'm reading.

• • • • • • • • • •

The picture shows a big creature that looks like a man, but it's covered with hair and is much bigger than a human. Now I understand what those two men saw.

In 1955, a trapper named William Roe said he spotted Big Foot near a deserted gold mine in Alberta, Canada. This time, Big Foot was crouched on the ground, eating the leaves off some branches. Roe says that Big Foot was as surprised to see him as he was surprised to see the monster. As it walked into the trees, Roe reports, Big Foot made a strange noise. It sounded like a combination of laughing and talking.

In 1958, a crew building a road in northern California found footprints of Big Foot near Bluff Creek. Big Foot had been circling the crew's equipment! More footprints were found there in August of 1967. It was just two months later that Patterson took his famous film of Big Foot there. Between 1964 and 1970, Big Foot was seen 25 times. In 1973, a photographer took another picture of it.

As recently as 1987, an oil crew working in British Columbia reported seeing Big Foot. About 7 feet tall and weighing about 400 pounds, it seemed more like a man than a monster. It watched the crew closely, and curiously. It also left giant footprints in the snow 6 feet apart. **?** *Strategy Alert!*

Stop and Ask **?**

If it doesn't make sense, what can I do? Use the photos and illustrations to help me understand what I'm reading.

I looked at the picture on page 154 and saw what William Roe must have seen.

Finding Family Members

Is the Yeti part of the same family as Big Foot? The Yeti reportedly lives high in the snowy mountains of the Himalayas and is as tall as 16 feet. Sometimes the Yeti walks on two feet and sometimes on four. Hairy, smelly, long-armed, and bad-tempered, the Yeti has been glimpsed mostly at night. According to legend, whoever looks into the Yeti's glowing red eyes will die. Still, many Yeti footprints have been photographed by people who lived to show the pictures to others. ❓ *Strategy Alert!*

Stop and Ask ❓

If it doesn't make sense, what can I do? Use the photos and illustrations to help me understand what I'm reading.

. . . .

This creature doesn't look friendly at all! I definitely would not want to meet him face to face.

Identifying Big Foot

Is Big Foot simply a large bear? Bears are huge, hairy, and smelly. They live in the wooded areas of the northwestern United States and Canada. However, few bears can walk on two feet for more than a few steps.

Is Big Foot a gorilla, an ape, or another kind of **primate**? No primates except humans live outside of zoos in the United States or Canada. Gorillas do live in the mountains of central Africa, but they could not survive on the icy slopes of the Himalayas.

Some people now think that the smaller, timid Almas may actually be a group of ancient people who have managed to survive in the mountains. However, this theory does not explain the Yeti or Big Foot. There have been thousands of sightings of Big Foot and many casts of its footprints. Could these huge, deep footprints be faked without leaving other footprints in the snow or dirt?

At least two dozen organizations are devoted to finding evidence of Big Foot. They publish newsletters, operate Web sites, and follow up on reported sightings. They have tried for decades to answer the question, "Is Big Foot real or imagined?"

primate (prie·mayt)— humans, apes, monkeys, and their relatives

Now read the habit and strategy for **After I Read**. Then read my notes below.

After I Read

Which **HABIT** will I learn?
React to what I've read.
If I develop this habit, I will take time to think about what I've just read. Deciding what I think and what I feel helps me remember it better.

Which **STRATEGY** will I use to learn this habit?
Think about the similarities and differences between what I've just read and other things I have read.

My Notes

- Strategy says to think about the similarities and differences between what I've just read and other things I have read.
- I've read other articles and stories that tell about Big Foot.
- Some of them said the same things about Big Foot's size and the size of its footprints.
- But I've never read about anyone being kidnapped by Big Foot. That was different.

Now it's time to practice the three habits and strategies you learned when you read "In Search of Big Foot." Reread the habit and strategy below and then do it!

Before I Read

Which **HABIT** will I practice?
Think about what I know about the subject.
If I develop this habit, I will bring to mind what I already know about the subject. This gets me ready to connect what I read to what I know so I will understand it better.

Which **STRATEGY** will I use to practice this habit?
Look at the photos and illustrations and decide what I know about what they show.

 Use the **Before I Read Strategy Sheet** for "Watching for Water Monsters" on page 42 in the *Strategy Practice Book* to help you think about what you know about the subject.

Watching for Water Monsters

Do monsters live in certain lakes? Read on, and then decide for yourself.

People have told stories about the Loch Ness [lahk **nes**] monster since A.D. 565. That year, a priest named Saint Columba reported seeing a giant water beast in Loch Ness, Scotland. (*Loch* is Scottish for "lake.") The monster, now called Nessie, is said to be about 20 feet long, dark brown or black, scaleless, and hairless. Nessie is often described as having a head like an eel or a snake. The head is attached by a long, slender neck to a thick body. The body has three humps that sometimes show above the water. Some people report seeing front flippers. Some say they have seen horns.

Remember the *Strategy Alerts!* in **While I Read** in the last selection? They reminded you to use the photos and illustrations to help you understand what you're reading. Now do the same thing with this selection.

While I Read

Which **HABIT** will I practice?
Stop and ask, "If it doesn't make sense, what can I do?"
If I develop this habit, I will stop and figure out what to do so what I'm reading makes sense. Then I can keep reading and not be lost.

Which **STRATEGY** will I use to practice this habit?
Use the photos and illustrations to help me understand what I'm reading.

Use the **While I Read Strategy Sheet** for "Watching for Water Monsters" on page 43 in the *Strategy Practice Book* as you read.

tropical (**trah**·pi·kuhl)—very warm, in the area around the equator

prehistoric (pree·his·**tor**·ik)—from before events were recorded

plesiosaur (**plee**·see·oh·sahr)—a reptile dinosaur that lived in water and ate fish

Every year since the 1930s, an average of 7 sightings of Nessie have been reported. Some people wonder if Nessie is actually a family of sea monsters. Loch Ness is large: 1 mile wide and 24 miles long. It's 800 feet deep in places. Almost anything could hide in that much water.

Could Nessie be a large eel? That's not likely, because eels live in **tropical** water. The water at the bottom of Loch Ness is only about 40°F.

Could Nessie be a **prehistoric** creature that has managed to survive this long? Nessie does look like a **plesiosaur,** with its huge body, long neck, small head, and flippers. Yet how could plesiosaurs live for 60 million years without us seeing more of them? Also, this ancient creature was cold-blooded, like a snake. It depended on the heat of its surroundings to survive. It could not have survived in the chilly waters of Loch Ness.

Does Nessie exist? No one knows for sure. Still, every day people wait and watch beside Loch Ness, hoping for a glimpse of her.

 *Strategy Alert!*

Stop and Ask ❓

If it doesn't make sense, what can I do? Use the photos and illustrations to help me understand what I'm reading.

Other Lakes, Other Monsters

The United States has water monsters, too. A creature named Champ is said to live in Lake Champlain [shamp•**layn**]. This lake extends from northern New York State to Vermont. The monster was first spotted in 1609 by the French explorer Samuel de Champlain, for whom the lake is named. Since then, it has been seen about 250 times. Like Nessie, Champ is huge: about 25 to 30 feet long, with a small head and a long neck. It is reportedly able to hold its head 15 feet above the water.

Another monster, Chessie, is said to live in Chesapeake Bay in Maryland. Chessie was filmed for three minutes in 1982 as it swam in shallow water. Experts viewed the tape at the Smithsonian Institution in Washington, D.C., but they did not reach any conclusions about Chessie's existence.

❓ *Strategy Alert!*

Stop and Ask ❓

If it doesn't make sense, what can I do? Use the photos and illustrations to help me understand what I'm reading.

In 1983, 5 members of a highway construction crew watched a large creature wading near the shore of San Francisco Bay. It was 100 feet long but very thin and dark, like an eel. As the crew watched, it turned and swam out to sea. Some said it had two humps and others saw four. Three days later, a group of people was surfing 400 miles south of San Francisco Bay. They described the same monster. One surfer said it was only 10 feet from his surfboard!

Monsters have also been sighted off the California shore near Santa Barbara. They have been seen in Lake Folsom in California, Flathead Lake in Montana, Lake Walker in Nevada, Bear Lake in Utah, Lake Payette [pay•yet] in Idaho, and Lake Memphremagog [mem•fri•may•gahg] in Vermont.

Of course, Canada has monsters, too. A water monster named Ponik [poh•neek] was first spotted in a lake in Quebec [kwuh•bek] in 1873. In the 1970s, divers took a picture of a dark shape about 25 feet long. Ogopogo [oh•goh•poh•goh], the Snake in the Lake, lives in Lake Okanagan [oh•kuh•nah•guhn] in British Columbia. Supposedly, if you cross this lake in a boat, you had better throw live animals overboard to feed the monster. In 1968, Ogopogo was briefly filmed. It seemed to be 60 feet long and 3 feet wide.

Stop and Ask ?

If it doesn't make sense, what can I do? Use the photos and illustrations to help me understand what I'm reading.

? *Strategy Alert!*

Water Monsters Around the World

South Americans also tell tales of water monsters. Nahuelito [nah•wel•**ee**•toh] is a monster that lives in Lake Nahuel Huapí [nah•**wel** wah•**pee**] in southern Argentina. During the summer, Nahuelito suddenly surfaces in a spray of water. Some say this monster is 15 feet long. Others insist it's 10 times longer. It's described as a giant water snake with humps.

There are also water monsters in the African Republic of Congo. As big as a hippopotamus, these monsters have long necks and tails. With their clawed feet, they can attack canoes.

In the 1970s, Swedish scientists used baby pigs as bait to try to catch a water monster. The monster reportedly lives in a lake in central Sweden. It was first seen more than 350 years ago, but it has been seen 500 times since 1987. It is red with a white mane and can move up to 45 mph. It may be 10 to 45 feet long. (The bait did not work, by the way. The monster is still free.) **?** *Strategy Alert!*

Stop and Ask ?

If it doesn't make sense, what can I do? Use the photos and illustrations to help me understand what I'm reading.

Real or Imagined?

Water monsters have also been sighted in Iceland, Norway, Ireland, England, and Australia. Can all these people be mistaken? Are all these sightings actually waves, or large fish, or shadows, or floating logs—or deliberate hoaxes, meant to trick people? What do you think?

> Remember that you're not finished until you've reacted to what you've read.

After I Read

Which **HABIT** will I practice?
React to what I've read.

If I develop this habit, I will take time to think about what I've just read. Deciding what I think and what I feel helps me remember it better.

Which **STRATEGY** will I use to practice this habit?

Think about the similarities and differences between what I've just read and other things I have read.

 Use the **After I Read Strategy Sheet** for "Watching for Water Monsters" on page 44 in the *Strategy Practice Book* to help you react to what you've read.

Apply 3 of the 9 Habits

Now read "Strange Rains" and apply these three habits and strategies.

Before I Read

Which **HABIT** will I apply?
Think about what I know about the subject.

Which **STRATEGY** will I use to apply this habit?
Look at the photos and illustrations and decide what I know about what they show.

While I Read

Which **HABIT** will I apply?
Stop and ask, "If it doesn't make sense, what can I do?"

Which **STRATEGY** will I use to apply this habit?
Use the photos and illustrations to help me understand what I'm reading.

After I Read

Which **HABIT** will I apply?
React to what I've read.

Which **STRATEGY** will I use to apply this habit?
Think about the similarities and differences between what I've just read and other things I have read.

 Use the **Self-Assessment Sheet** for "Strange Rains" on pages 45–46 in the *Strategy Practice Book* as you read to see how well you can apply the habits and strategies.

Strange Rains

You know that rain, snow, hail, and sleet often fall from the sky. According to some reports, so do frogs, fishes, snakes, and other living things! Below are some accounts of small animals raining from the sky. Many of these strange rains were reported by magazines and newspapers that are known for printing factual material.

1841 An English magazine called *The Athenaeum* [a·thuh·**nay**·uhm] reported:

> During a heavy thunderstorm, the rain poured down in torrents mixed with half-melted ice, and, incredible as it may appear, hundreds of small fishes and frogs in great abundance descended with the torrents of rain. The fish were from half an inch to two inches long. Many were picked up alive. The frogs jumped away as fast as they could, but the **bulk** of them were killed by the fall on the hard pavement.

bulk (buhlk)—the biggest part or large amount

1859 In Wales, which is part of the British Isles, a man named John Lewis caught some of the fish that suddenly showered down on a small area around him. Some of the fish were still alive, so he gave them to a zoo aquarium, where they were exhibited. Scientists at the British Museum, however, believed that someone had simply tossed a bucket of fish on Lewis.

1873 *Scientific American* published this account in its July 12 issue:

> A shower of frogs, which darkened the air and covered the ground for a long distance, is the reported result of a recent rainstorm in Kansas City, Missouri.

1883 *The Decatur Daily Republican* newspaper printed this article:

> Cairo, Illinois, August 3. Early yesterday morning the decks of the steamers *Success* and *Elliot*, **moored** at the Mississippi **levee,** were observed to be literally covered with small green frogs about an inch in length, which came down with a drenching rain which prevailed during the night. Trees and fences were literally alive with the slimy things.

moored (moord)—kept in place by cables, lines, or anchors

levee (lev•ee)—a river landing place

1887 Another article from *Scientific American* reported on a rain of snakes in Memphis, Tennessee:

> Thousands of little reptiles, ranging from a foot to 18 inches in length, were distributed all over the southern part of the city.

1939 The English journal *Meteorological Magazine* described this strange rain:

> Mr. E. Ettles, superintendent of the municipal swimming pool, stated that about 4:30 p.m. he was caught in a heavy shower of rain and, while hurrying to shelter, heard behind him a sound as of the falling of lumps of mud. Turning, he was amazed to see hundreds of tiny frogs falling on the concrete path around the bath. Later, many more were found to have fallen on the grass nearby.

1947 A biologist working for the United States Department of Wildlife and Fisheries witnessed an unusual event in Marksville, Louisiana. His report was published in the magazine *Science*. Here is part of it:

> In the morning of October 23, 1947, between seven and eight o'clock, fish ranging from two to nine inches in length fell on the streets and in the yards. I was in the restaurant with my wife having breakfast, when the waitress informed us that fish were falling from the sky. We went immediately to collect some of the fish. The director of the bank said that he had discovered that fish had fallen by hundreds in his yard, and in the adjacent yard. The cashier of the bank and two merchants were struck by falling fish as they walked toward their places of business about 7:45 a.m. Automobiles and trucks were running over them.

1972 In its March issue, *Australian Natural History* described 54 different rains that had contained fish and a few that had included frogs. All took place between 1879 and 1971.

1994 Between 1988 and 1994, three major fish falls were recorded in the Australian desert. After heavy rains, thousands of small, live fish flopped around in the sand and on nearby parking lots and roads. Some fish swam in puddles left by the storms.

Explaining Fish and Frog Falls

With so many reports, is it possible that sometimes it rains frogs or fishes? How could this happen? One theory is that a tornado or other storm sucked the tiny animals into the air, perhaps pulling them out of a pond or lake. Then it carried them a long distance and dropped them in a different area. Yet why would a tornado pick up just one kind of animal? And why would it pick up only animals that were all about the same size?

Dr. William Hayden Smith, Professor of Earth and Planetary Science at Washington University in St. Louis, Missouri, can explain why the fish or frogs that fall are nearly the same size. The winds probably pick up some adult frogs or large fish, plus thousands of young frogs or fish. Being heavier, the adults soon fall, but no one notices. However, the young frogs or fish are lighter and can be carried farther by the winds. When thousands of them fall, people notice!

Are these strange rains real or imagined? Just to be safe, look outside the next time it rains. You can never be sure of what you will see!

Put Your Habits to Work in

Literature	Social Studies	Science	Math

Before I Read Habit:
Think about what I know about the subject.

Look at the photos and illustrations as a way of thinking about what you know about this topic. Connecting what you're going to read with what you already know will help you understand it better.

While I Read Habit:
Stop and ask, "If it doesn't make sense, what can I do?"

As you go along, use the photos and illustrations to help you understand what you're reading by connecting to what you already know.

After I Read Habit:
React to what I've read.

Take time to think about the similarities and differences between what you've just read and other things you've read.

I thought about . . .

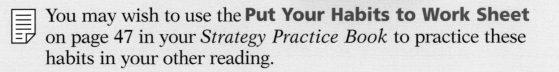

You may wish to use the **Put Your Habits to Work Sheet** on page 47 in your *Strategy Practice Book* to practice these habits in your other reading.

Unit 8
Dreamers and Adventurers
Theme: People

In this unit, you will develop these 3 habits for all readers.

Before I Read Habit:
Decide what I need to know.

While I Read Habit:
Stop and ask, "Does it make sense?"

After I Read Habit:
Check to see what I remember.

Learn 3 of the 9 Habits

In this unit, you will work on three habits—one for before you read, one for while you are reading, and one for after you finish reading. Start with **Before I Read**. Read the habit and strategy. Then read my notes below.

Before I Read

Which **HABIT** will I learn?
Decide what I need to know.
If I develop this habit, I will have a reason for reading. I will understand it better and remember more of what I read.

Which **STRATEGY** will I use to learn this habit?
Use the headings to decide what the author will tell me.

My Notes

- Strategy says to use the headings to decide what the author will tell me.

- From looking at the headings, it looks like a story about going up or climbing something.

- There are some unfamiliar words. I will look for their meanings in the story.

- The last heading talks about a dream. I want to read to find out whose dream it was and what the dream was about.

Reaching the Peak

Mount Everest

What is the highest place you've ever been? Maybe you've been high in the Rocky Mountains or on the **observation deck** of the Sears Tower in Chicago. Those are pretty high places, but compared to the highest point on Earth they seem very small. The highest point on Earth is the top of Mount Everest, on the border of Tibet [ti•**bet**] and Nepal [nay•**pahl**] in Asia. It is 29,028 feet tall reaching nearly 5½ miles into the sky. You can get to the top of the Sears Tower (1,800 feet high) by walking into an elevator and pushing the "up" button. Getting to the top of Mount Everest is a lot harder. That's what Sir Edmund Hillary and Tenzing Norgay found out. They were the first people to reach the peak and return to tell about their adventure.

observation deck
(ahb•zur•**vay**•shuhn dek)—an area near the top of a tall building for looking out

Now read the habit and strategy for **While I Read**. When you see ❓, read my notes in the margin.

While I Read

Which **HABIT** will I learn?
Stop and ask, "Does it make sense?"
If I develop this habit, I will stop now and then to make sure I understand what I'm reading.

Which **STRATEGY** will I use to learn this habit?
I can answer the author's questions.

Ruapehu
(roo•uh•**pay**•hoo)—the highest mountain in New Zealand

expedition
(ek•spuh•**di**•shuhn)—a journey undertaken for a specific purpose, often an adventure or scientific mission

Stop and Ask ❓

Does it make sense? I can answer the author's questions.

• • • • • • • • • • •

Hillary was a mountain climber from New Zealand and Norgay supervised an expedition to climb Mt. Everest. It makes sense that they became friends, because they did something dangerous together.

Who Were Hillary and Norgay?

Sir Edmund Hillary was born in New Zealand in 1919. His family raised bees and farmed. New Zealand has many mountains, but Hillary's family was busy making a living. It wasn't until he was 16 years old that Hillary first saw a mountain, Mount **Ruapehu** north of Wellington [**wel**•ing•tuhn], the capital of New Zealand. It was love at first sight. He loved the snow. He loved the challenge of the climb. He loved the feeling of freedom he got standing at the top of a mountain peak. From then on, Hillary climbed whenever he could. Right after World War II, he and Harry Ayres climbed Mount Cook in New Zealand. They were the first to climb that peak's southern ridge.

Less is known about Tenzing Norgay. Norgay supervised the **expedition** to climb Mount Everest. He and Hillary became good friends. ❓ *Strategy Alert!*

The Sherpas

Norgay was a Sherpa, one of a group of people who have always lived in the Himalayas, the mountain chain where Mount Everest is located. Without the knowledge and strength of Sherpa guides and assistants, climbing Mount Everest would probably be impossible.

Climbers working their way up Mount Everest

Have you ever tried to carry a heavy box up a hill or up a flight of stairs? If so, then you know how strong the Sherpas must be to carry supplies up the world's highest mountain. Sherpas lay the trail and carry supplies in an area so high that no motor-powered vehicles, such as trucks, can function. A motor needs **oxygen** to mix with fuel and cause combustion to get it started and keep it working. There's not enough oxygen at the top of Mount Everest to do this. Even helicopters are unable to fly there. The air is so thin that the blades have nothing to push against to keep the helicopter in the sky. The power behind an **ascent** of Everest is muscle power.

🛑 *Strategy Alert!*

Climbing Everest

When he was in his early thirties, Hillary took part in many climbing expeditions in the Himalayas. All were in preparation for an attempt on Mount Everest. In 1953, the attempt was made. A British expedition was going to make the climb. It took weeks of hiking just to get to Everest. Several hundred **porters** carried gear. At about 13,000 feet, they crossed the tree line, the point where it is so high that trees can no longer grow. There is nothing to provide shelter from the wind and cold.

oxygen (**ahk**•si•juhn)— the part of the air that your body uses to stay alive

ascent (uh•**sent**)—an upward movement or climb

Stop and Ask ❓

Does it make sense? I can answer the author's questions.

• • • • • • • • • • • •

Yes, I have tried to carry heavy boxes up some stairs. I was tired and out of breath by the time I got to the top. Now I understand how strong the Sherpas need to be to carry supplies up the mountain.

porters (**por**•turz)— persons hired to carry equipment and supplies

The Nuts and Bolts—Or Ropes and Crampons

How does climbing a tall mountain affect your body? At a high **altitude,** the oxygen in the air thins out, making it difficult to breathe. Snowy slopes and icy cliffs rise up in front of you, making it difficult to find and keep a foothold. The temperature drops drastically to many degrees below zero and fierce winds whip around you. These were the challenges Hillary and his group faced. They could fall, freeze to death, die of **altitude sickness,** or simply wander off, never to be seen again. **?** *Strategy Alert!*

The team rests on the long trek up Mount Everest.

That's what happened to climbers George Mallory and Andrew Irvine on their expedition in 1924. No one knows whether they reached the top. They simply disappeared. Seventy-five years later, in 1999, Mallory's frozen body was found. From the place where he died, many climbers think that he did not reach the top, but a clear answer has not yet been found. If Mallory and Irvine did reach the peak, it would mean that Hillary and Norgay were not the first people to stand on the top of Everest. The history books—and this article—would have to be rewritten.

Everything about the expedition had to be planned with great care, from the route to take up the mountain to the number of oxygen tanks to carry. Special gear, such as crampons and ice axes, was used. Crampons are sharp spikes that attach to climbing boots. They give climbers a better grip on ice and snow. Ropes are tied carefully between climbers and anchored to handholds and rocks to keep climbers from falling. Ice axes are used to chip handholds in the ice. Climbers also use ice axes to stop themselves if they start sliding down a field of snow. Digging in with the point of the ax slows climbers down enough to get back on their feet.

A climber uses crampons and ice axes to climb these snow covered peaks.

Making the Ascent

Slowly, the climbers worked their way across the icefall, a dangerous glacier. They set up 8 camps above the icefall, each at a higher altitude. They would climb from one camp to the next, resting at each one for several weeks to allow their bodies to get used to the new, higher altitude. This phase of the climb took months.

From Camp 8, two-person teams would try to reach the top of the mountain. Hillary and Norgay were to be the second team to make the attempt. How did they get to be the first to try for the top? It happened when the first team's oxygen tanks failed to operate. Suddenly, Hillary and Norgay had the chance to be the very first to see the world from its highest point, from the top of Mount Everest. On May 29, 1953, from a camp even higher than Camp 8, they started out. ❓ *Strategy Alert!*

Stop and Ask ❓

Does it make sense? I can answer the author's questions.

. . . .

I know that they got their chance when the first team's oxygen tanks didn't work. That makes sense, because the story said how important oxygen is.

oxygen masks—masks
that are connected to a
tank of oxygen; used to
assist in breathing in
places where there is not
enough oxygen

summit (sum•uht)—the
top of a mountain

Wearing **oxygen masks** and crampons, they climbed over snow and ice. They came to a 40-foot cliff and Hillary almost turned back. They had to get to the **summit** and back as quickly as possible, and his legs felt as heavy as iron. But his dream of reaching the peak spurred him on. He wedged himself between the ice and the cliff and slowly crept up the crack an inch at a time. Finally, he was out of the crack! But ahead of him was more ice! Would they ever reach the topmost point? Trudging across the ice, Hillary became aware that it was starting to slant down instead of up. They had made it to the peak. Hillary and Norgay shook hands, planted a flag, took some pictures—and then got down from there as quickly as they could!

A Dream Fulfilled

What did Edmund Hillary do after he made his dream come true? He dreamed more dreams and worked to make them come true. He continued climbing for many years. He made a trip across Antarctica to the South Pole. He toured the world, telling people about his adventures. He also worked hard and raised a lot of money to help the people of Nepal and Tibet build schools, hospitals, roads, and airstrips. There are many controversies today about climbing Mount Everest, but no one questions Hillary and Norgay's **momentous** accomplishment. ❓ *Strategy Alert!*

momentous
(moh•**ment**•uhs)—
important

Stop and Ask ❓

Does it make sense? I can answer the author's questions.

• • • • • • • • • • • •

After I read it once, I couldn't answer the question, so I read this part again. I found out he explored and helped people in Nepal and Tibet. He kept on dreaming, and I guess that makes sense.

Hillary and Norgay

Now read the habit and strategy for **After I Read**. Then read my notes below.

After I Read

Which **HABIT** will I learn?
Check to see what I remember.
If I develop this habit, I will check to see what I remember as soon as I finish reading. It helps me see if I really understood what I read and helps me remember it better, too.

Which **STRATEGY** will I use to learn this habit?
Decide what the teacher might ask me.

My Notes

- Strategy says to decide what the teacher might ask me.
- I'll think of questions the teacher might ask on a quiz.
- Some questions might be: How high is Mount Everest? Where was Edmund Hillary born? Who were the Sherpas? What equipment is needed to climb a mountain?
- Other questions might be: What is altitude? How did Hillary and Norgay get to make the first attempt when they were supposed to be second? What did Hillary do after he became the first to reach the top? Why did Hillary want to climb mountains?
- If I can answer these questions, I'll know that I really understood what I read.

Now it's time to practice the three habits and strategies you learned when you read "Reaching the Peak." Reread the habit and strategy below and then do it!

Before I Read

Which **HABIT** will I practice?
Decide what I need to know.
If I develop this habit, I will have a reason for reading. I will understand it better and remember more of what I read.

Which **STRATEGY** will I use to practice this habit?
Use the headings to decide what the author will tell me.

Use the **Before I Read Strategy Sheet** for "Earhart's Adventures" on page 48 in the *Strategy Practice Book* to help you decide what you need to know.

Earhart's Adventures

Amelia Earhart

"The captain has turned off the seat belt sign. Feel free to move around the cabin." This is about as exciting as air travel gets for most people. They strap into seats and arrive where they're going so smoothly that it doesn't feel much like flying. Things were different for Amelia Earhart. Earhart, who disappeared mysteriously in 1937, was a pilot in the early days of **aviation**. She flew in open planes. She could feel the wind stream past her face and see the earth rush up to meet her when she landed. She spent half of her life following her dreams of flying.

aviation
(ay•vee•**ay**•shuhn)—the operation of heavier-than-air aircraft

Remember the *Strategy Alerts!* in **While I Read** in the last selection? They reminded you to answer the author's questions. Now do the same thing with this selection.

While I Read

Which **HABIT** will I practice?
Stop and ask, "Does it make sense?"
If I develop this habit, I will stop now and then to make sure I understand what I'm reading.

Which **STRATEGY** will I use to practice this habit?
I can answer the author's questions.

Use the **While I Read Strategy Sheet** for "Earhart's Adventures" on page 49 in the *Strategy Practice Book* as you read.

The Dream Is Born

Earhart was a pioneer of aviation. She was born in Atchison, Kansas, on July 24, 1897. She loved adventure and travel even when she was a young girl. One story tells of how Earhart and her sister built a roller coaster on the roof of a shed. The crash landing didn't bother her a bit! Have you ever tried anything so daring?

 Strategy Alert!

Earhart graduated from high school in Chicago in 1915. Soon after that, she traveled to Toronto, Ontario, where she worked as a nurse's aide during World War I (1914–1918). That's where Earhart's dream of being a pilot was born. She went to college for a little while, but the dream of flying was stronger than her dream of becoming a doctor. She left college and moved to California. In California, she worked at a telephone company to pay for flying lessons and saved enough money to buy her own airplane.

Stop and Ask **?**

Does it make sense? I can answer the author's questions.

Earhart's Plane

Have you ever flown in an airplane? You may have flown in a large jet that seated hundreds of people. But the single-engine planes in which Earhart learned her piloting skills were small, **fragile** machines. They were built of metal or wood frames that were covered with canvas or sheet metal. The cockpit, the part of the plane holding the pilot, was open to the sky. Pilots wore heavy jackets, goggles, and scarves to protect themselves from the open air.

❓ *Strategy Alert!*

fragile (**fraj**·uhl)—easily broken or destroyed

Stop and Ask ❓

Does it make sense? I can answer the author's questions.

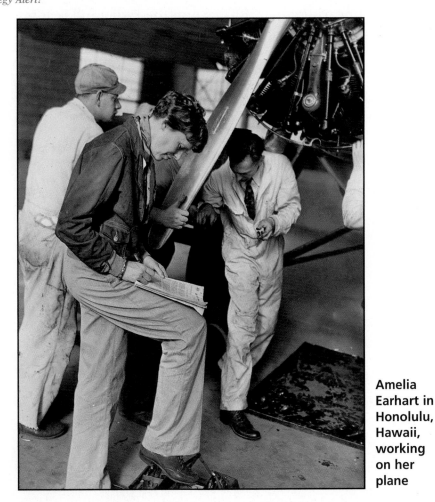

Amelia Earhart in Honolulu, Hawaii, working on her plane

Airplane technology changed rapidly during Earhart's flying career. Technology is the application of knowledge in a particular area, in this case, aviation. Earhart kept up with the technology. By the end of her career, she was flying in closed-cockpit planes with a radio and a navigator on board. These airplanes could fly much farther and faster than the earlier planes.

Aviation Excitement

Flying by itself wasn't enough for Earhart. She wanted to set and break records. One after another, she set new challenges for herself and met them. Many of her records were women's records.

At that time, most airplane pilots were men. By setting records and writing books about her adventures, Earhart opened up the field of aviation for women. She was well known around the world. She also gave **inspiration** to people around the world who were suffering through the hard **economic** times of the **Great Depression**. They liked hearing about Earhart on the radio and reading about her in the newspaper.

inspiration
(in•spuh•**ray**•shuhn)—a vision of hope and achievement

economic
(ek•uh•**nah**•mik)—related to money and finances

Great Depression—the hard times in the 1930s when many people were out of work and the future was uncertain

solo (**soh**•loh)—by one-self; in aviation, a flight with only the pilot in the plane

Does it make sense? I can answer the author's questions.

The mayor of New York City awards Amelia Earhart a medal following a parade in her honor.

Setting Records

What records did Earhart set? Her first record, set in 1928, was being the first woman to fly across the Atlantic Ocean as a passenger. That same year, however, she also set a record as a pilot. She became the first woman to make a **solo** round-trip flight across the United States. In 1929, she came in third in the very first Women's Air Derby. In 1930, she set a women's speed record: 181.19 miles an hour. *Strategy Alert!*

In 1932, Earhart became the first woman to fly across the Atlantic Ocean solo. In 1933, she broke her own **transcontinental** record, flying the distance in 17 hours, 7 minutes, and 39 seconds. That seems slow today, but for the 1930s it was a very fast trip.

Some of Earhart's records were records for men and women. In 1935, she became the first person to fly over the Pacific Ocean from Hawaii to California. Also that year, she was the first person to fly from Los Angeles to Mexico City, Mexico, and from Mexico City to Newark, New Jersey.

transcontinental
(trans•kahnt•n•ent•l)
—from one side of a continent to the other

What Happened to Earhart?

In 1937, Earhart set off in search of yet another accomplishment. She wanted to fly all the way around the world staying as close to the equator as possible. By this time, Earhart was famous. News reporters and photographers tracked every part of her journey. People around the world were watching and listening to stories about Earhart's trip.

Earhart speaks with reporters following her record-breaking transcontinental flight.

On May 20, 1937, Earhart and her **navigator,** Fred Noonan, took off from Oakland, California, flying east. Their route was well planned, with many stops for rest and refueling. On July 2, flying from New Guinea to Howland Island in the Pacific, Earhart radioed her position. Then she was never heard from again. Her plane may have crashed into the ocean, and sunk, or it may have been lost forever in a dense jungle on an island. No one knows. Legends have persisted about her disappearance. There have been many reports of sightings of the wreckage of her plane. But neither her plane nor her body has ever been found. ⑦ *Strategy Alert!*

navigator
(**nav**•uh•gay•tur)—the crew member who is in charge of keeping the plane on course

Stop and Ask ⑦

Does it make sense? I can answer the author's questions.

Dare to Dream

Do you have a dream? Is there something you want to do so much that nothing will slow you down? It's easy to focus on Earhart's daring, but she worked hard, too, in following her dream. She said, "If you find something that you want to do, then do it. If you want to try a certain job, try it. . . . It may turn out to be fun, and fun is an important part of work." Dreams take work, courage, and the willingness to take risks. Amelia Earhart's life was a combination of all of these. The events surrounding her disappearance are still a mystery, but her spirit lives on in anyone who dares to dream.

Strategy Alert!

Stop and Ask ?

Does it make sense? I can answer the author's questions.

Remember that you're not finished until you've checked to see what you remember.

After I Read

Which **HABIT** will I practice?
Check to see what I remember.
If I develop this habit, I will check to see what I remember as soon as I finish reading. It helps me see if I really understood what I read and helps me remember it better, too.

Which **STRATEGY** will I use to practice this habit?
Decide what the teacher might ask me.

Use the **After I Read Strategy Sheet** for "Earhart's Adventures" on page 50 in the *Strategy Practice Book* to help you check to see what you remember.

Apply 3 of the 9 Habits

> Now read "Pole Position" and apply these three habits and strategies.

Before I Read

Which **HABIT** will I apply?
Decide what I need to know.

Which **STRATEGY** will I use to apply this habit?
Use the headings to decide what the author will tell me.

While I Read

Which **HABIT** will I apply?
Stop and ask, "Does it make sense?"

Which **STRATEGY** will I use to apply this habit?
I can answer the author's questions.

After I Read

Which **HABIT** will I apply?
Check to see what I remember.

Which **STRATEGY** will I use to apply this habit?
Decide what the teacher might ask me.

 Use the **Self-Assessment Sheet** for "Pole Position" on pages 51–52 in the *Strategy Practice Book* as you read to see how well you can apply the habits and strategies.

Roald Amundsen

Pole Position

In 1911, a great international contest took place. Two expeditions raced to be the first humans ever to reach the South Pole. One team was **British,** led by Robert Scott. The other team was a group of **Norwegians**. Whose flag would be planted at that **frigid,** forbidding spot? The story of the Norwegian team centers on the expert planning of Roald Amundsen [**roh**·ahl **ahm**·uhn·suhn]. Amundsen, an experienced **polar** explorer, was the leader of the Norwegian expedition.

Robert Scott

British (**brit**·ish)—from the country of Great Britain

Norwegians (nor·**wee**·juhnz)—people from the country of Norway

frigid (**frij**·uhd)—very, very cold

polar (**poh**·lur)—having to do with Earth's North or South Pole

A Way of Life

How did the race to the poles begin? The Norwegian expedition's journey to the South Pole did not begin at a base camp and not on the day they set sail from Norway. It began in Amundsen's lifelong **urge** to explore, discover, and compete. Amundsen, who was born in 1872, grew up in Oslo, Norway. His family owned a fleet of ships. He spent his childhood learning about ships and sailing. He heard stories of faraway places. When Amundsen was away from the water, he spent time skiing. In Norway, which is located far north of the equator, it is snowy and icy much of the time. In those conditions, cross-country skiing is a necessity as well as a sport. Amundsen became a strong skier. These two influences, ships and skis, figured in all of Amundsen's adult **endeavors**.

urge (urj)—a continuing desire to do some particular thing

endeavors (in•**dev**•urz)—serious, determined efforts

Roald Amundsen's vessel

Dreams of Polar Exploration

Amundsen dreamed of polar exploration. How did his choices lead toward that goal? He learned as much as he could. In 1894, he went on his first sea voyage in the northern Arctic Sea, as a mate aboard a ship called the *Magdelena*. On that journey and many others, he gathered information and gained physical strength. He studied how the **Inuit** and other people **indigenous** to cold regions survived, including learning about their sleds and dogs.

In 1896, Amundsen made his first long journey to the Antarctic, the region surrounding the South Pole. Serving on a ship called the *Belgica* [bel•**jee**•kah], he learned everything he could, by having many conversations with another expedition member, Frederick Cook.

What were some of the things Amundsen learned? He learned how equipment and fur clothing worked in polar conditions. Part of the *Belgica's* mission was to become frozen in the ice on purpose for several months. Amundsen learned about the physical, mental, and nutritional needs of people under those conditions. He learned how to prevent scurvy, a disease caused by a lack of certain vitamins in the diet. And, being Amundsen, he filed the information away for the day he would need it.

Inuit (**in**•yoo•it)—the people native to the Arctic

indigenous (in•**dij**•uh•nus)—having always lived in a place

Change of Poles

What do you think Amundsen did next? He selected the North Pole as his target. However, as Amundsen was planning this expedition, he heard that the North Pole had been reached. In secret, Amundsen changed his plans. He decided to try for the South Pole instead. The secrecy was important because another expedition, Scott's expedition, was also heading for the South Pole. Amundsen did not want to speed them up with the news that they had a race on their hands.

The South Pole is the southern end of the earth's axis.

Race to the Pole

Amundsen's expedition arrived in Antarctica in 1911, aboard a ship called the *Fram*. The expedition included just 18 men, all experienced sled-dog drivers and skiers. They set up a base camp during January and February, the Antarctic summer. From the base camp, the team set up food and supply stations that were easy distances apart along the route they would follow to the pole. These reserves of hidden food were one of the most important parts of Amundsen's plan. Why was food so important to Amundsen? He made sure lots of food was available because he had seen hunger aboard the *Belgica* and did not want to see it again. On the way to the pole, the team traveling with dog sleds would leave food behind to eat on the return trip.

Amundsen's rival, Scott, took ponies instead of sled dogs and carried all of the food. Amundsen took dogs because he knew they were well adapted to the frozen conditions they would face. Who made the better choice? Amundsen did. All of Scott's ponies died. His party ended up hauling their sleds by hand.

Robert Scott prepares for his expedition.

The Long Winter

Amundsen's team worked as hard as they could during the short summer. As it got colder and darker, they moved inside. They built sleds, checked equipment, and made flags to mark their food reserves. They were trapped in camp by the weather until October 1911. Finally, Amundsen selected 4 men to make the run to the pole with him. On October 11, they set out with the dog sleds, leaving food in well-marked spots as they traveled.

Reaching the Pole First

The team traveled from a camp on the Ross Ice Shelf due south to the Axel Heiberg Glacier [**aks**·uhl **hie**·burg **glay**·shur]. They climbed the glacier and emerged onto a plateau [pla·**toh**], a wide, flat area of land. Travel on the bumpy plateau was difficult. The team was slowed by fog and blizzards. Soon, however, they reached a smoother area. By December 8, they were farther south than anyone had ever been before. Would they make it to the pole? Would they beat Scott's expedition?

At 3:00 on December 15, 1911, all of their instruments showed that they were there. The team had made it to the South Pole. As they looked around carefully and took extra readings, they could find no sign that anyone else had ever been there. They were the first. They had beaten Robert Scott to the pole. Excitedly, they planted a flag and took pictures. They pitched a tent for Scott to find and left a letter for him. They asked him to tell the King of Norway about their success if they did not survive the journey back to camp. On December 18, they headed back to base camp. Everyone made it back in good health.

What happened to Scott? Scott and the 4 members of his team had run out of food. Their ponies were dead. They reached the South Pole 33 days after Amundsen. Sadly, Scott and the men with him all died during the return trip from the South Pole.

The Norwegian expedition reaches the South Pole.

Sad Return Home

Amundsen's team left Antarctica on the *Fram* on January 30, 1912. A century later, people remember Scott, but cannot recall Amundsen's name. Amundsen went on to lead and participate in many other expeditions. He became the first person to see both the North and the South Poles, (although he only flew over the North Pole). His thoroughness and planning always served him well. He died in a plane crash at sea in 1928, attempting to rescue a friend.

Put Your Habits to Work in

Literature **Social Studies** **Science** **Math**

Before I Read Habit:
Decide what I need to know.

Look at the headings to decide what the author will tell you. This will help you know what to expect as you read the selection.

Light, Pollution, and Distortion

Galileo's telescope was revolu-

Light and air pollution are problems for modern astronomers. However, there is a third problem that Galileo also faced

Putting Hubble in Space

Edwin Powell Hubble lived from 1889 until 1953 and discov-

While I Read Habit:
Stop and ask, "Does it make sense?"

As you go along, stop every now and then to see whether it makes sense by trying to answer the author's questions.

A Brief History of the Hubble

Look up at the night sky and what do you see? You're sure to spot lots of stars, a few constellations, and maybe a couple of planets. With our

After I Read Habit:
Check to see what I remember.

Check on what you remember by writing down questions the teacher might ask you about the selection.

One question the teacher might ask is . . .

You may wish to use the **Put Your Habits to Work Sheet** on page 53 in your *Strategy Practice Book* to practice these habits in your other reading.

Unit 9
Westward Bound!
Theme: People on the Move

In this unit, you will develop these 3 habits for all readers.

Before I Read Habit:
Think about what I know about the subject.

While I Read Habit:
Stop and ask, "How does it connect to what I know?"

After I Read Habit:
Check to see what I remember.

In this unit, you will work on three habits—one for before you read, one for while you are reading, and one for after you finish reading. Start with **Before I Read**. Read the habit and strategy. Then read my notes below.

Before I Read

Which **HABIT** will I learn?
> **Think about what I know about the subject.**
> If I develop this habit, I will bring to mind what I already know about the subject. This gets me ready to connect what I read to what I know so I will understand it better.

Which **STRATEGY** will I use to learn this habit?
> Skim the selection to see if I'm familiar with the setting.

My Notes

- Strategy says to skim the selection to see if I'm familiar with the setting.
- I skimmed it and saw that it's about a cowboy.
- Cowboy stories are set in the West.
- I think this story will be set in the West.

Bulldoggin' Bill

"**Lay-deez** and gentlemen, give a big Texas welcome to that bulldoggin' wizard of the West. Here's Bill Pickett, the **Dusky** Demon!" The rodeo announcer's voice boomed. The crowd cheered. A gate opened at one end of the arena, and out rode Bill Pickett on his best horse **Spradley**. The crowd continued to hoot and holler as Pickett trotted around the arena, waving his big old cowboy hat at the people who had come to see him.

People had come to see him. How did that happen? He was just a ranch hand who grew up selling vegetables. How did this crowd of people come to be cheering for him, an African American cowboy whose parents had been slaves?

lay-deez—ladies

dusky (**duhs**•kee)—dark, as in the evening

Spradley (**sprad**•lee)

Now read the habit and strategy for **While I Read.** When you see , read my notes in the margin.

While I Read

Which **HABIT** will I learn?

Stop and ask, "How does it connect to what I know?"

If I develop this habit, I will think about how what I'm reading fits with what I know. This helps me understand the new material and remember it better.

Which **STRATEGY** will I use to learn this habit?

See if I can picture the time when the events are taking place.

---

strides (striedz)—steps, or lengths of steps

furious (fyur·ee·uhs)— very angry

Stop and Ask ❓

How does it connect to what I know? See if I can picture the time when the events are taking place.

I can't really picture the time yet, but everything so far has been happening during a rodeo.

Action in the Arena

But this was no time for thinking. It was time for action. Another gate opened. A huge bull with angry eyes and big, sharp-pointed horns came thundering into the arena. Pickett and Spradley knew just what to do. They galloped around in a curve and came up alongside the bull. Horse hooves and bull hooves thundered in the dirt, drowning out the sound of the crowd in Pickett's ears. As the horse and bull matched **strides,** Pickett took a leap into the air. He leaped across the space between his horse and the bull, landing right on the bull's back! The **furious** bull snorted and bucked.

Pickett wrapped his arms around the bull's horns, twisting its head back until he and the bull were face to face. Then he sank his teeth right into the bull's upper lip! The bull was so shocked that he dropped to the ground. The people in the crowd went crazy. Bill Pickett had done it again. He had wrestled a bull and won!

❓ *Strategy Alert!*

Life and Times of the Rodeo

Nobody thought up rodeos. They began in the late 1800s. They started out as **informal** contests among cowboys, with other cowboys as the only audience. Gradually these contests became events. People from surrounding farms and towns would hear about the cowboys' skills and come out to watch. Cowboys would "pass the hat" and the **spectators** would toss in a few coins for the winners. Then somebody thought of charging people to watch. Some cowboys were so good that they were able to earn a living as rodeo riders. That's how the rodeo was born. Today rodeos travel all over the world, entertaining millions of people.

A cowboy wrestling a steer at a rodeo

Steer Wrestling

Bulldogging is the rodeo event that made Bill Pickett famous. He invented it. One day he saw a bulldog bring down a cow by biting and holding onto its lip. The cow stopped struggling instantly when its lip was bit. Young Pickett just had to try it, too! Bulldogging, or **steer** wrestling, as it is now called, is one of the 7 events in professional rodeos. (The other 6 are saddle bronc riding, bareback riding, bull riding, calf roping, team roping, and barrel racing.)

? *Strategy Alert!*

---

informal
(in•**for**•muhl)—casual, not organized

spectators
(**spek**•tay•turz)—people who are watching

steer —in cattle, a male animal not able to produce young

Stop and Ask **?**

How does it connect to what I know? See if I can picture the time when the events are taking place.

• • • • • • • • • • •

The late 1800s was a long time ago. I can picture people on horses riding out to watch cowboys do tricks.

A cattle drive

Life and Times of Bill Pickett

Bill Pickett was born somewhere near Austin, Texas, around 1870. No one knows the exact date or place of his birth. The West was still pretty wild then, and people didn't take time to stop and keep records. Pickett's father, Thomas, had come to Texas from South Carolina in the 1850s. He was a slave and had to go where his master went. In 1865, however, slavery ended for all African Americans and Thomas Pickett was free. He met Mary Gilbert. They married, bought a piece of land, and began raising a family. Bill Pickett was the second of their 13 children.

herding (hurd·ing)— moving animals in a group

The family farmed and sold their crops of vegetables. But young Bill could never seem to pay any attention to farming. He was more interested in cowboys. His family lived near one of the main trails for taking cattle to market. Groups of cowboys would ride by, **herding** thousands of cattle along the trail in what was called a cattle drive. The cow that the bulldog bit was probably from one of these herds. ❓ *Strategy Alert!*

Stop and Ask ❓

How does it connect to what I know? See if I can picture the time when the events are taking place.

I have seen movies with cattle drives. I can picture the cattle, the horses, and the dust of a cattle drive in the Old West.

Becoming a Cowboy

Pickett had a deep interest in cowboys. He also had uncles who were cowboys. So, it's no surprise that when he was 15 years old, Pickett set out on a cowboy career of his own. There were many African American cowboys in the Old West. Many had moved west with former masters and stayed after they became free, like Thomas Pickett. Other African Americans had moved west on their own, to take advantage of the opportunities that were not open to them back east. Good workers were valuable. Most ranchers didn't make decisions based on the color of someone's skin. If you were a good worker, you had a job.

Rodeo Years

Pickett worked as a cowboy and ranch hand off and on, but his skill as a bulldogger soon gave him a new career. Wherever Pickett was working, people would come around to watch him wrestle steers to the ground. Soon he began performing in rodeos and shows and finally became a full-time rodeo rider. One day, the owner of a huge ranch, the 101 Ranch in Oklahoma, hired Pickett to **tour** with his rodeo, the famous 101 Ranch Wild West Show. Bill Pickett and Spradley became the stars of the show. ? *Strategy Alert!*

tour (toor)—to go on organized travel

Stop and Ask ?

How does it connect to what I know? See if I can picture the time when the events are taking place.

My family went to a rodeo last year, so I can picture what it must have been like.

Cowboys in early Oklahoma

Pickett traveled all over the world with the 101 Ranch Wild West Show. But in 1916 he went home. He was tired. He wanted to spend time with his family. He never stopped working with horses though, and kept in good bulldoggin' shape. Sadly, though, in 1932 he was kicked by a wild horse on the 101 Ranch in Oklahoma. He died from those injuries.

inducted
(in•**duhk**•tid)—placed

Hall of Fame—a
place that honors
famous people in a
certain field and dis-
plays pictures and
items they used during
their lives

heritage
(**hair**•uh•tij)—things
shared from the past

The Hall of Fame

In 1971, Pickett was **inducted** into the National Cowboy **Hall of Fame** and Western **Heritage** Center in Oklahoma City. He is now listed in the Rodeo Hall of Fame of this museum. That's good. That means his life and his deeds—and his bulldoggin'—will live on for a good long time. Bill Pickett, the Dusky Demon, and his horse Spradley will be remembered for years to come.

Now read the habit and strategy for **After I Read**. Then read my notes below.

After I Read

Which **HABIT** will I learn?
Check to see what I remember.
If I develop this habit, I will check to see what I remember as soon as I finish reading. It helps me see if I really understood what I read and helps me remember it better, too.

Which **STRATEGY** will I use to learn this habit?
Summarize the selection.

My Notes

- Strategy says to summarize the selection.
- That means I should write some sentences that tell what the selection was all about.
- My summary says, "Bulldoggin' Bill was Bill Pickett. He was a famous rodeo rider who was born around 1870 and died in 1932. He lived in Texas. He invented a rodeo event called steer wrestling. In 1971, he was inducted into the National Cowboy Hall of Fame."

Now it's time to practice the three habits and strategies you learned when you read "Bulldoggin' Bill." Reread the habit and strategy below and then do it!

Before I Read

Which **HABIT** will I practice?
Think about what I know about the subject.
If I develop this habit, I will bring to mind what I already know about the subject. This gets me ready to connect what I read to what I know so I will understand it better.

Which **STRATEGY** will I use to practice this habit?
Skim the selection to see if I'm familiar with the setting.

Use the **Before I Read Strategy Sheet** for "The Story of Stagecoach Mary" on page 54 in the *Strategy Practice Book* to help you think about what you know about the subject.

The Story of Stagecoach Mary

Back when I was a girl, around the early 1900s, there was a woman in our town like no one I had ever met before. And in all the long years I've lived, I've never met another like her. She was very old when I was a child, and famous in our town, which was Cascade, Montana. Her name was Mary Fields. We called her "Stagecoach Mary."

Just Mary Fields

Mary Fields was so famous in Cascade that her birthday was a holiday. We always got the day off from school and that was reason enough to like her. But no one really knew when Mary's birthday was. One year we celebrated it twice! Stagecoach Mary did lots of things no one had ever seen a woman do before, and she did them well. Mary did exactly what she wanted to do. Nobody messed with Mary.

Remember the *Strategy Alerts!* in **While I Read** in the last selection? They reminded you to see if you can picture the time when the events are taking place. Now do the same thing with this selection.

While I Read

Which **HABIT** will I practice?
Stop and ask, "How does it connect to what I know?"

If I develop this habit, I will think about how what I'm reading fits with what I know. This helps me understand the new material and remember it better.

Which **STRATEGY** will I use to practice this habit?
See if I can picture the time when the events are taking place.

Use the **While I Read Strategy Sheet** for "The Story of Stagecoach Mary" on page 55 in the *Strategy Practice Book* as you read.

Tennessee Times

Stagecoach Mary was born in Tennessee in 1832. She was born into slavery and no one knows what her early years were like. But somewhere along the way she learned the skills that made her famous—the ability to shoot straight, drive a team of horses, work hard, and keep her word. And somewhere along the way, she grew to be six feet tall, the tallest woman I ever saw, and 200 pounds strong. But she wasn't Stagecoach Mary, yet.

Montana Move

In 1865, African Americans were given their freedom, including Mary. Somehow, she made her way north to Toledo, Ohio, where she was working for a Catholic nun in 1881. The nun, Mother **Amadeus** [ah•muh•**day**•uhs], was asked to move from Toledo to St. Peter's Mission, 8 miles outside of Cascade, Montana. A few years later,

Mother Amadeus wrote to Mary back in Toledo and offered her a job hauling supplies for the mission. Mary Fields took her up on the offer. In 1884, she moved to Montana. She was still just Mary Fields, but not for long.  *Strategy Alert!*

Mary and the Wolves

For 8 years, Mary worked for St. Peter's Mission. She drove wagons loaded with supplies back and forth between the mission and the town. She smoked a big cigar and carried a rifle and a pistol. Nothing was going to happen to the supplies while Mary was in charge.

My folks told me the story of Mary and the wolves. It was a dark, dark night. Mary was late getting back to St. Peter's. Nearby, she heard howling. Then, she heard growling. Suddenly, a blur of gray—several blurs of gray—came flying out of the woods. Wolves! The horses **shied and reared** and broke their **traces**. Off they went, galloping to safety. The wagon tipped, spilling bags, boxes, and barrels onto the road.

But what about Mary? Mary was quick. She fired the pistol, then the rifle, frightening the wolves back a few yards. Quickly, she gathered **sagebrush** from the sides of the road and lit a blazing fire to keep the wolves away.

When the town was just waking up, in came Mary. She had loaded the supplies back onto the wagon and came **trudging** into town, hauling that wagon herself. She was stubborn and she was strong. She made sure no wolves would get her supplies.

 *Strategy Alert!*

Stop and Ask ?

How does it connect to what I know? See if I can picture the time when the events are taking place.

shied and reared—in horses, backed up with the front legs in the air

traces (**tray**•suhz)—the parts of a harness that attach a horse to a wagon

sagebrush (**sayj**•bruhsh) —a shrubby plant that grows in the western plains

trudging (**truh**•jing)— walking with slow, heavy steps

Stop and Ask ?

How does it connect to what I know? See if I can picture the time when the events are taking place.

Stagecoach Mary at Last

Mary was friendly—unless she was crossed. She had many adventures and did things no one had ever seen a woman do before. She became a legend around Cascade. The bishop up at Helena, Montana, started hearing things about her, good and bad. One day, she challenged a man to a shoot-out. Well, that was too much for the bishop. Mary was out of a job. For a while, she ran a restaurant, but it went out of business fast. Mary kept giving away food. She couldn't turn away anyone who was hungry. Meanwhile, she got the job that gave her the nickname that stuck. She got a job driving the town's stagecoach. In 1895, in her sixties, Mary Fields finally became Stagecoach Mary.

A stagecoach was a closed wagon with seats inside. It was pulled by four horses or more. Stagecoaches carried people, supplies, and the mail. Stagecoach Mary was only the second woman in the United States to carry the mail. And she was the first African American woman to do it. Whether people liked Mary or not didn't matter. What mattered was that she could be trusted with important letters and packages. If anyone could get the mail through, it was Stagecoach Mary Fields.

? *Strategy Alert!*

Stop and Ask **?**

How does it connect to what I know? See if I can picture the time when the events are taking place.

Stagecoach Mary's Laundry

When Stagecoach Mary was in her seventies, she started yet another career. She felt too old to drive, so she started a laundry business. That's what she was doing when I was a child. I remember the day she knocked out a customer. He hadn't paid for his laundry and that made Mary angry. One day, when she was at the hotel, she saw him pass by. She went right outside and knocked him out cold with her fist. When she came back inside, she said, "Well, that bill's settled." That was one of the last stories about Mary. She died in 1914.

Stagecoach Mary's Legend

Stagecoach Mary lives on in **legend** now, but she was a real, flesh-and-blood woman. You can still see her grave in the Hillside Cemetery in Cascade—at least you could the last time I was there. The town loved her. The hotel gave her all of her meals free. And when the laundry burned down, the whole town pitched in with free **lumber** and free labor. She was back in business in no time. For a long time, a **portrait** of her hung in one of the banks in Cascade. Every time I saw it I smiled. Stagecoach Mary was tough. She lived life exactly the way she wanted to. She didn't worry about what people thought of her. But do you know what they thought of her? They thought she was a great woman. **?** *Strategy Alert!*

legend (**lej**•uhnd)—a story that came down from the past

lumber (**luhm**•bur)— wood that has been sawed into boards

portrait (**por**•truht)— a painting of a person

Stop and Ask **?**

How does it connect to what I know? See if I can picture the time when the events are taking place.

> Remember that you're not finished until you've checked to see what you remember.

After I Read

Which **HABIT** will I practice?
Check to see what I remember.
> If I develop this habit, I will check to see what I remember as soon as I finish reading. It helps me see if I really understood what I read and helps me remember it better, too.

Which **STRATEGY** will I use to practice this habit?
> Summarize the selection.

 Use the **After I Read Strategy Sheet** for "The Story of Stagecoach Mary" on page 56 in the *Strategy Practice Book* to help you check to see what you remember.

Now read "Riding for the Pony Express" and apply these three habits and strategies.

Before I Read

Which **HABIT** will I apply?
Think about what I know about the subject.

Which **STRATEGY** will I use to apply this habit?
Skim the selection to see if I'm familiar with the setting.

While I Read

Which **HABIT** will I apply?
Stop and ask, "How does it connect to what I know?"

Which **STRATEGY** will I use to apply this habit?
See if I can picture the time when the events are taking place.

After I Read

Which **HABIT** will I apply?
Check to see what I remember.

Which **STRATEGY** will I use to apply this habit?
Summarize the selection.

 Use the **Self-Assessment Sheet** for "Riding for the Pony Express" on pages 57–58 in the *Strategy Practice Book* as you read to see how well you can apply the habits and strategies.

Riding for the Pony Express

Wanted:

❧❀❧

*Young,
skinny,
wiry fellows
not over 18.*

❦

**Must be expert riders
willing to risk death daily.**

ORPHANS PREFERRED

————————

Wages: $25.00 a week.

Who would want a job like that? What kind of company would ask its employees to risk death? Read on to learn why hundreds of young men wanted this job. You will find out why only eighty riders were chosen and what they were asked to do. You will also learn how they became legends in only 18 months!

The Need for News

By the spring of 1860, half a million people were living in the new states of Oregon and California. They had traveled there by horse, mule, covered wagon, and stagecoach. There were no airplanes and no cars. Train tracks went no farther than the Missouri River. The first tracks to cross the nation would not be completed for nine years.

Most of the people living on the west coast had gone there hoping to find gold. However, they still wanted to stay in touch with their families back east. They had also heard rumors about a possible civil war. They were desperate for news.

Yet they had no televisions, radios, or telephones. Telegraph lines could send messages long distances by **Morse code**. However, like the train tracks, these lines stopped at the Missouri River. People could send letters from the east coast to the west coast on ships. However, the trip all the way around South America often took six months!

Morse code (mors kohd) —a way of sending messages using a system in which letters and numbers are represented by dots and dashes or long and short signals

Making Promises

Sending mail overland seemed like a better idea. Starting in 1858, Congress paid a stagecoach company to carry mail between St. Louis, Missouri, and Sacramento, California. The long route curved south through Texas and New Mexico. The stagecoaches made the 2,800-mile trip twice a month. The trip took three weeks each way. That was much faster than sending mail on a ship. However, people still did not want to wait that long for news.

William Russell and his two partners had run a successful **freight** company for years. The company used wooden wagons pulled by oxen. The wagons carried tons of materials across the Great Plains and the Rocky Mountains. In 1860, Russell talked his two partners into starting a new company, the Pony Express. Riders on speedy horses would carry mail and news overland.

Russell and his partners decided on a route that was different from the one the stagecoaches took. The riders would travel directly west. This route would be "only" 2,000 miles long. However, it crossed the Sierra Nevada Mountains. The owners knew this route would be difficult in winter. Still, Russell promised that their riders could deliver mail in ten days. Even his partners were not sure they could meet that goal.

freight (frayt)—goods carried by vessel or vehicle

This postage stamp shows a Pony Express rider and a map of the 2,000-mile route.

Getting Started

The new company needed riders and horses. Hundreds of young men answered the advertisement you read earlier. However, Russell and his partners chose only 80 of the best riders. They selected small, strong, brave men. Few of them weighed over 120 pounds. A heavy man would slow down his horse.

The average horse cost about $50 back then. However, the Pony Express did not want average horses. At the eastern end of the route, the company paid up to $200 for a horse. Like the men, the horses had to be small, strong, and brave. Short legs would help them on the slippery mountain slopes.

At the western end of the route, many of the horses were mustangs. Mustangs are wild horses, known for their strength, speed, and intelligence. They were caught for the Pony Express. However, there was no time for taming and training. For some horses, the first person to sit on their backs was the Pony Express rider. The first part of his ride was like a rodeo. The mustang often tried to buck the rider off!

The Pony Express bought about 500 horses. They lived in **stables** at 120 **stations** along the route. When it was time for a rider to come by, the station man got a fresh horse ready. The rider would jump off his sweaty horse and onto the fresh one. This switch might take only 15 seconds. The rider also moved the mail pouch, called a **mochila,** to his new horse.

Then the rider would take off at a **gallop**. He stopped for nothing. Seconds counted in the tight schedule. After riding about 15 miles, he came to another station. There, he changed horses again. Each rider changed horses 5 to 7 times and rode 75 to 100 miles. Then he passed the mochila to the next rider.

stables (stay•blz)— buildings used to house horses

stations (stay•shuhnz)— stopping places along the route of the Pony Express

mochila (moh•chee•luh)—a leather bag used by the riders to carry the mail

gallop (gal•uhp)—a very fast run

Riding Into History

The Pony Express ran 24 hours a day. The determined riders were able to complete the 2,000-mile route in 10 days or less. They galloped across burning deserts. They picked their way through icy mountain passes. Often they had to outrun robbers.

The robbers knew the mail might contain gold or money. In addition, Native Americans often chased riders who crossed their land. One rider was shot in the forehead with an arrow, but he survived. "Willing to risk death daily" was truly part of the job. Yet only one man died while riding for the Pony Express.

The riders quickly became heroes. Crowds cheered them as they galloped through towns. People liked to tell about one rider who was only 14 years old. One day, he was trapped in a canyon by robbers. One robber reached for the mochila. The rider grabbed the other end and threw it at the robber's face. The rider escaped with his life and the mail. His name was Billy Cody. Now he is known as Buffalo Bill Cody.

Another time, Cody pulled his sweating horse to a stop at a station. They had just traveled 116 miles. But Cody learned that the next rider had died the night before. He jumped onto a fresh horse. They carried the mail another 76 miles to the next station. There, a fresh rider took over. Cody headed back to his home station. He rode 384 miles, stopping only to change horses.

The horse of another rider, George Little, died in a fierce snowstorm. Little stuffed the mail into his shirt. Then he walked to Salt Lake City. He was 16 years old at the time. Stories like these are part of the legend of the Pony Express.

The End of the Ride

On October 24, 1861, the first telegram was sent from San Francisco to Washington, D.C. Crews in Salt Lake City had just connected telegraph wires that linked both coasts. Two days later, the Pony Express closed. There was no longer a need for it. News traveled much faster by telegraph. In fact, the Pony Express had been losing money during its entire 18-month run. Russell and his partners were broke.

The riders had galloped 600,000 miles. They had carried 34,752 pieces of mail. More importantly, they had helped make the west coast part of our new nation. The United States had many challenges ahead as it entered the Civil War. However, the daring riders of the Pony Express helped build a nation that could meet those challenges.

Put Your Habits to Work in

Literature | **Social Studies** | **Science** | **Math**

Before I Read Habit:
Think about what I know about the subject.

Skim the selection to see if you're familiar with the setting.

> Chester walked through the parlor with his skating boots slung over his shoulder. It was December 1873, the day after a night cold enough to freeze the Sandy River solid. His three broth-ers and two sisters had already gone out. Only his parents and his grand-mother were in the room.

How Chester Greenwood Invented Earmuffs

While I Read Habit:
Stop and ask, "How does it connect to what I know?"

As you go along, stop every now and then to try to picture the time when the events are taking place.

> When Chester went back outside to skate, his friends laughed at him. He didn't pay any attention. At last his ears were warm. The afternoon grew colder, but Chester skated on. Finally, he was the only one left on the ice. His friends, their ears cold, had been forced to go in.

After I Read Habit:
Check to see what I remember.

Check on what you remember by summarizing the selection.

> This selection tells . . .

You may wish to use the **Put Your Habits to Work Sheet** on page 59 in your *Strategy Practice Book* to practice these habits in your other reading.

Habits and Strategies

Use this chart to review the 9 good habits and the strategies you have been using. If you want, review the strategies by looking back at the unit.

Before I Read

1. **Check it out!**
   - Skim the charts or graphs to see what it's about. (Unit 1)
   - Identify the genre. (Unit 5)
   - Skim the summary and predict what the selection will be about. (Unit 6)

2. **Think about what I know about the subject.**
   - Use the headings to decide what I know about this topic. (Unit 3)
   - Look at the photos and illustrations and decide what I know about what they show. (Unit 7)
   - Skim the selection to see if I'm familiar with the setting. (Unit 9)

3. **Decide what I need to know.**
   - Use the headings to ask purpose-setting questions. (Unit 2)
   - Use the genre to decide what might happen in the story. (Unit 4)
   - Use the headings to decide what the author will tell me. (Unit 8)

While I Read

4. **Stop and ask, "How does it connect to what I know?"**
   - Think about whether I've ever done something similar. (Unit 3)
   - Design a graphic organizer. (Unit 5)
   - See if I can picture the time when the events are taking place. (Unit 9)

5. **Stop and ask, "Does it make sense?"**
   - Decide whether what I'm reading fits with what I know about the topic. (Unit 1)
   - Decide if what's happening fits with the genre. (Unit 4)
   - I can answer the author's questions. (Unit 8)

6. **Stop and ask, "If it doesn't make sense, what can I do?"**
   - Use context clues to help me understand the meanings of unknown words. (Unit 2)
   - Slow down when the reading gets difficult. (Unit 6)
   - Use the photos and illustrations to help me understand what I'm reading. (Unit 7)

After I Read

7. **React to what I've read.**
   - Create a graphic organizer of what I've read. (Unit 2)
   - Decide whether I like the main character or not. (Unit 4)
   - Think about the similarities and differences between what I've just read and other things I have read. (Unit 7)

8. **Check to see what I remember.**
   - Answer the questions in the text. (Unit 6)
   - Decide what the teacher might ask me. (Unit 8)
   - Summarize the selection. (Unit 9)

9. **Use what I've read.**
   - Identify the most important ideas. (Unit 1)
   - Decide what I thought was interesting. (Unit 3)
   - Tell what I learned about the central character. (Unit 5)